Everyday Life
in Colonial Maryland, Delaware, Pennsylvania and Virginia

By George and Virginia Schaun

Cover Design By Graphica, Inc. of Lanham

Sixteenth Revised Edition, January, 1996.

(First Edition, October, 1959)

Published by

Maryland Historical Press

9205 Tuckerman Street,
Lanham, MD 20706-2777

This latest edition of North American colonial life, January 1996, has been expanded from its original format to include information on colonial life not only in Maryland but that of the adjoining colonies of Delaware, Pennsylvania and Virginia. The original title of Everyday Life in Colonial Maryland has been changed to Everyday Life in Colonial Maryland, Delaware, Pennsylvania and Virginia.

The editor of this edition is Vera Foster Rollo, Ph. D., working in conjunction with Virginia Schaun. George Schaun, who died in 1988 at the age of 87, had used many sources in Virginia, Delaware and Pennsylvania when he, with Virginia Schaun, wrote the first editions and published them under the aegis of their Greenberry Press of Annapolis.

Copyright © 1996
Maryland Historical Press

ISBN 0-917882-41-5

Library of Congress Cataloging-in-Publication Data

Schaun, George.
    Everyday life in colonial Maryland, Delaware, Pennsylvania, and Virginia
    / by George and Virginia Schaun. -- 16th, rev. ed. p.   cm.
    Rev. ed. of: Everyday life in colonial Maryland. 15th ed. 1980.
    Includes bibliographical references and index.
    ISBN 0-917882-41-5 (alk. paper)
    1. Maryland--Social life and customs--To 1775. 2. Virginia--Social life and
    customs--To 1775. 3. Pennsylvania--Social life and customs--To 1775. 4.
    Delaware--Social life and customs--To 1775.
    I. Schaun, Virginia. II. Schaun, George. Everyday life in colonial
    Maryland. III. Title.
    F184.S33 1996
    975.2'02--dc20
                                                                    95-33283
                                                                         CIP
                                                                          AC

CONTENTS

EVERYDAY LIFE IN COLONIAL MARYLAND

Chapter   **Page**

ABOUT THE AUTHORS

George and Virginia Schaun of Annapolis, Maryland, began publishing texts for school and library use in 1956 under the firm name, Greenberry Publications. In the following 21 years they published 21 texts.

George Schaun studied at the Peabody Conservatory of Music and has served as the music critic of the *Baltimore Sun,* and music editor of the *Sunday Sun.* During World War II, he worked as civilian historian of the Signal Corps. After the war he became Assistant Manager and Program Annotator of the Baltimore Symphony Orchestra.

He has served as editor and publisher of several respected Maryland periodicals and has written many articles on Maryland. During its founding years, 1953-1955, he served as the first Executive Director of *Historic Annapolis, Inc.*

Virginia Schaun is a graduate of the Philadelphia School of Occupational Therapy and practiced in that field for thirteen years. After her marriage she came to Annapolis, in 1953, to work as Tour Bureau Director and Craft Shop Manager for *Historic Annapolis.*

Virginia Schaun is the author of articles in *The Maryland Conservationist* and other Maryland periodicals. With George Schaun she researched, helped to write, illustrate and print the Greenberry Press publications for over 20 years.

The Schauns write in a vivid, informative style, about many facts and factors on Maryland not discussed elsewhere. The Schauns have a fresh and sometimes unexpected focus of attention. The writers delved into primary source materials in Annapolis and elsewhere to give their work a scholarly foundation.

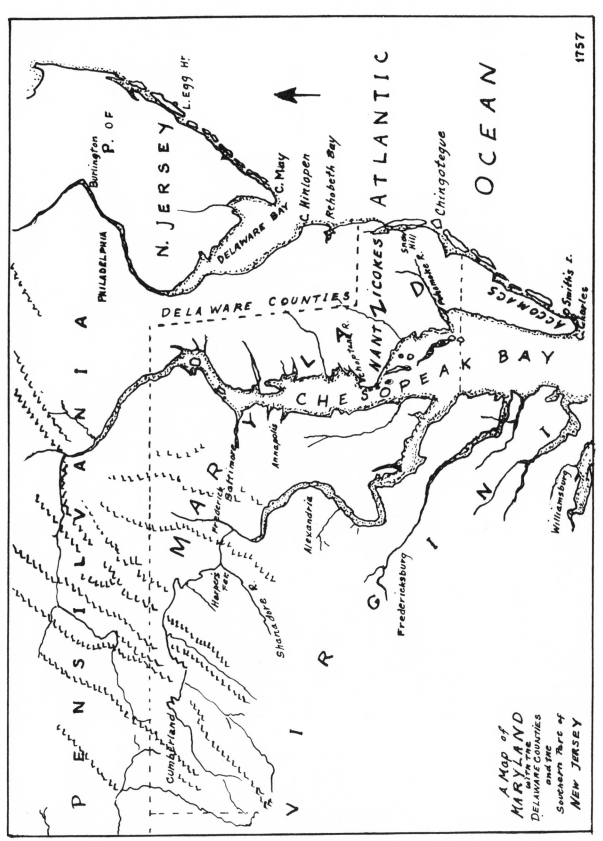

This sketch is derived from a map drawn in 1757 which shows the relative locations of Maryland, the "Delaware Counties," Pennsylvania and Virginia. Many names were spelled differently from present spelling. For example, the Allegheny Mountains were then known as the "Endless Mountains."

THE THIRTEEN COLONIES

1 7 6 3

ILLUSTRATIONS

In the Carroll County Farm Museum this young woman shows us how spinning wheels were used to make thread for weaving. Can you see two modern things in the photograph that colonial ladies would not have known about? J. H. Cromwell photo.

Chapter 1

How People Lived

Life in the 18th-century mid-Atlantic colonies, some books say, seems to have been a time of riding in sedan chairs or coaches, eating delicious foods such as fried chicken, canvasback duck, or soft-shell crabs; drinking much Madeira, Port, or other expensive imported wines; of fox hunting, dancing, going to the theatre and the races; and living, in general, far better than any king.

After reading other comments, one might be impressed by the lack of comforts and "conveniences," as well as by the difficulties experienced by most colonists merely in earning a living.

Which is correct? The truth lies between the two extremes. Members of the upper class, consisting mainly of plantation owners and other wealthy individuals, lived well. They enjoyed many pleasures and depended upon slaves or paid servants for the performances of most farm or household work. They were educated, as a general rule. Yet they were only a small part of the total population.

The great majority of those living in the colony, from the early 1700's until the American Revolution, consisted of low-income working people and their families; indentured servants; and black slaves. Making a living was not always an easy matter, and people had few of what we would call luxuries. Amusements were simple ones, more or less "home-made," such as "quilting bees," dancing, "taffy pulling," playing cards or other games, fishing and hunting.

Indentured Servants

In those days, therefore, life depended a great deal upon one's occupation, education, social position, and wealth. The term "indentured servant," for example, usually referred to a person who, in exchange for a sum of money or for passage on a ship to America, signed an agreement (known as an "indenture") to work as a servant for four or five years. Frequently, this arrangement offered the only means whereby those who had little money could pay for the long, dangerous, and expensive voyage by sailing vessel from the Old World to the frontiers of the New World. Sometimes, those who did not have enough money to pay for a passage overseas were taken aboard, but were allowed a certain length of time, after arrival, to earn enough money to pay the ship captain. These people were called "redemptioners."

Before rubber hoses and cast-iron waterpipes came into use,
this was one way of hauling water from one place to another.

Built-in bathtubs and plumbing were unknown in the 18th century. Hot water poured into a wooden tub, on Saturday nights
(or perhaps less often), provided the bathing facilities
used by everyone.

How People Lived (cont'd)

William Buckland

Then, as now, lack of money did not necessarily indicate lack of either talent or ambition. On the contrary, many of these indentured servants were educated, and some were highly skilled. One of them, William Buckland, has become famous among architects and others who admire beautiful buildings. He designed such remarkable colonial dwellings as Gunston Hall, near Lorton, Virginia (first of the houses he designed in America), and the Hammond-Harwood House (the last house he designed), in Annapolis. Now open to the public as museums, these two buildings--- and various others--- attract many visitors. They come from considerable distances, each year, to admire the products of Buckland's genius as an architect.

Another notable person of colonial Maryland, Ninian Beale (1625-1717), was a Scot who had been captured by Cromwell's men and then shipped to America as a prisoner. Nevertheless, after "serving his time," he became influential and prosperous enough to patent 25,000 acres of land.

These two illustrate the fact that indentured servants, who had special ability, training, and character could rise to positions of prominence. Much in demand were:

"Mill-wrights, Ship-wrights, Boate-wrights,
Wheel-wrights, Brick-makers and Bricklayers,
Joyners, Master Carpenters and Architects,
Coopers, Turners, Sawyers,Smiths, Cutlers,
Millers," and so on.

There were some indentured servants, of course, who did not turn out well. After serving the agreed period, some turned to begging and drinking, wandering about from one community to another, and doing as little work as possible. Others were put in jail or punished in other ways for their wrong doing. Generally speaking, however, most of them became useful and respected citizens. Some served as schoolmasters and teachers. Many of them are counted as honored ancestors, nowadays, by a considerable number of our leading citizens.

Freedom Dues

After serving for the agreed period of time, indentured servants were usually entitled to "freedom dues," intended to help them get along successfully in their new life as "freemen." Sometimes, as in Buckland's case, they were even paid a small salary. The right to collect the "freedom dues" was well protected by the law courts, as shown by existing legal records telling about action taken to collect them. For example, an indentured servant named Henry Spenk sued the heirs of his master for "freedom dues" consisting

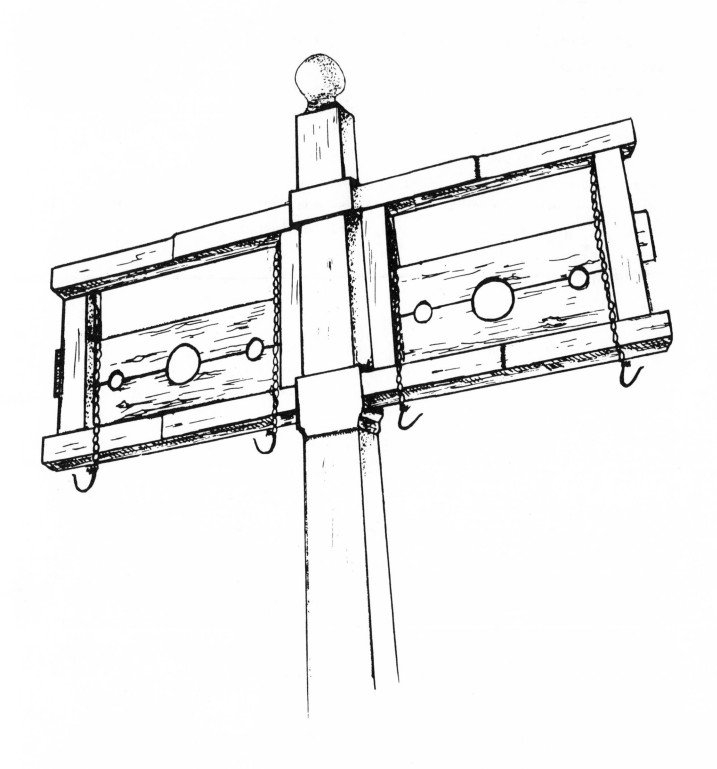

PILLORY (for two people)

How People Lived

of "one cap or hatt, one cloak or frize suit, one shirt, one pair shoes &
stockins, one broad and one narrow hoe, 50 acres of land, and 3 barrells
Corne."

> (A decision of the Provincial Court, in 1648, specified almost
> these exact items as "freedom dues" in Maryland. Beginning in
> 1683, "freedom dues" of the Province no longer included a
> tract of land, and there were other alterations in later years).

Slave Labor

Many planters preferred to have black slaves as laborers because once a
slave was bought the planter then had a lifetime worker, with no further
expenses for either wages or "freedom dues." Furthermore, children born to
married slaves also became the property of the slave-owner, increasing his
number of workers without additional cost except for food, clothing, and
incidentals.

For somewhat similar reasons, most colonists wanted large families of
their own. Every child soon became a worker of one sort or another. On a
farm, there were many tasks that could be performed by a youngster.

Apprentices

Parents frequently signed agreements under which their sons, in their
"pre-teens" or "early teens," became apprentices. In this way, boys
learned how to earn a living and received an education at the same time,
without cost. As an apprentice, a boy lived in the household of a craftsman (the master of some trade, such as printer, shoemaker, or wheelwright).
There he learned a trade by assisting his master in doing his work. The
bargain usually provided that the master workman would also teach his
apprentice how to read and write. Room and board were supplied but no
wages were paid. After working and taking lessons for five, six, or seven
years, the boy became a "journeyman" and, as such, was qualified to accept
employment at regular wages or else to set up a business of his own.

> An inexpensive but interesting booklet, Apprenticeship, Past and
> Present (pub. by U.S. Department of Labor as No. 0-351585) may be
> obtained from the Superintendent of Documents, U.S.Gov't.Printing
> Office, Washington,D.C.,20025. It tells us, for instance, that the
> transfer of skills by apprenticeship was mentioned 2100 B.C. in the
> Babylonian Code of Hammurabi, which stated that artisans should
> "teach their crafts to youth."
>
> It also describes accomplishments of Paul and Thomas, who served
> in Colonial Massachusetts as apprentices under their father, a
> French Huguenot immigrant named Apollos Rivoire. That name may
> mean little until we realize that it was changed somewhat. Paul,
> around the world, is extremely well remembered as Paul Revere. His
> famous ride was only one incident in a busy life during which he

How People Lived (Cont'd)

was a fine silversmith and coppersmith. He cast many church bells (some still ringing in various American cities); and started America's first copper-rolling mill (an ancestor of present-day Revere Copper and Brass Company).

On page 17 of this booklet, it tells of a man who asked each of three stone masons: "What are you doing?"

The first answered: "I am earning my living."
The second replied: "I am cutting stone to measure."
The third responded by saying: "I, sir, am building a cathedral!"

Convicts

Convicts, imprisoned in England (or other countries) for all sorts of offenses including inability to pay their debts, were often sent to America to work out their terms of sentence. After that, these, too, could enter into the free life of the colony and, by hard work and honesty, become respected citizens. Under severe laws of England, during the 17th century, the penalty for stealing a small sum of money was death--- and a judge could set the same penalty for tearing down a fence or stealing a sheep.

Many English judges were unwilling to impose such severe penalties. One way around the strict observance of the law was to give the convicted man his choice of being hanged, or of going to America as a bonded servant. Probably every one of them decided in favor of the trip to America! Upon arrival in an American port, these convicts were sold to anyone who wanted a servant or farm worker, working anywhere from seven to fourteen years before being granted freedom. (More serious crimes, such as murder, were punished in England by hanging). Pennsylvania, Virginia, and other colonies tried a number of times to stop this practice of sending convicts to America, but England would not agree to this. Many came to Maryland despite vigorous opposition by Governor Francis Nicholson and other governors who followed him. The Maryland General Assembly tried to block this practice, a number of times, but was always over-ruled by British authorities who found it a convenient solution to some of their problems.

Punishments

In Maryland, punishments were quite severe, too, as indeed they were in every part of the world at that time. There were not many jails and these had very little space. Frequently, the "lock up" for prisoners was actually the sheriff's own home, or some sturdy farm building provided with a strong lock. For convenience, Joseph Brunner, an early sheriff of Frederick County (at a place then called Schieverstadt) actually had some prison cells built

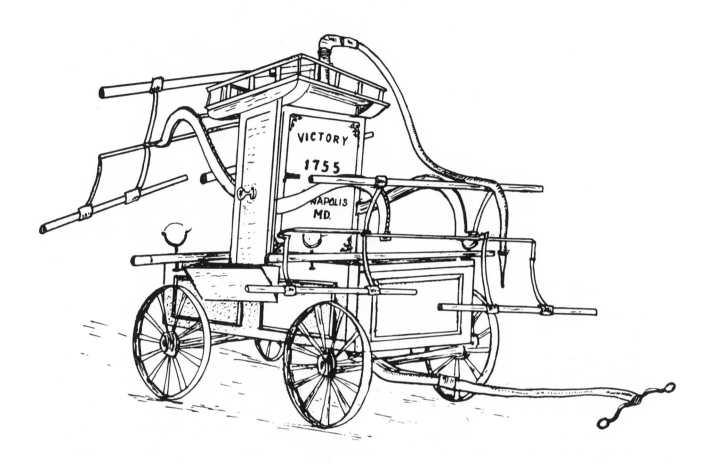

City of Annapolis

1708 · SETTLED · 1649 · ANNAPOLIS IN MARYLAND · SIGILL · IUSTITIA CRESCIT · CHARTERED · 1708 · 1958

ANNAPOLIS' FIRST FIRE ENGINE

"The Ancient City," [1887] By Elihu S. Riley, page 118, 1755 A. D., states:

"February 28th, was landed here from on board the Good, Captain Chew, for the use of the city, a very fine engine, made by New-them and Reagg, No. 1800, London, which the inhabitants last year generously subscribed for. It threw water 156 feet perpendicular." Was not this the city's present heirloom, "The Victory?"

Distributed on the occasion of the 250th Anniversary of the granting of the Charter to the City of Annapolis, November 22nd, 1958. Annapolis Charter Day Celebration.

How People Lived (Cont'd)

into the cellar of his home.

Because of the expenses and inconvenience of keeping prisoners in jail,
the authorities usually preferred to punish offenders by public whippings,
by putting them in the stocks or the pillory, (See page 4), by monetary
fines, or by branding (much dreaded because it was quite painful).Branding
left a permanent mark on the arm, cheek, or forehead, (a letter "T" to
mean "Thief," or letter "P" to mean "Perjurer," and so on). It was done by
means of an iron tool which had been heated in a fire.

It was not until 1674 that the General Assembly passed a law requiring
each county to provide a courthouse and a prison. Just outside each courthouse, as a rule, stood various devices for punishment--- such as a pillory,
a whipping-post, and a cage. Near these were the stone auction blocks on
which black slaves were compelled to stand, for public inspection, when the
auctioneer offered them for sale to the highest bidder. (A pillory usually
had a large hole for a man's head and two small holes so that he could be
fastened by the wrists. Held in this way, he would probably be an object
for ridicule, and perhaps a target for one or two overly ripe tomatoes.)

The pillory, the stocks, the branding iron, and the hangman's gibbet
did not disappear from use in Maryland until about 1810, when the peni-
tentiary system was adopted. Imprisonment for debt was not abolished in
Maryland until 1850. The last pillory and whipping-post was located near
the spot where Baltimore's Battle Monument now stands. A man was pilloried
there as late as 1819.

Selecting An Executioner

The position of Chief Executioner was not always easy to fill. A neat
solution to this problem was devised during Baltimore County's earlier
years (1660-1700). In the absence of other candidates for the job, the
life of a convicted murderer sometimes was spared on condition that he
carry out the task of executing others condemned to death. At various
times, the duties of executioner were assigned to someone who had been
sentenced to a long term of imprisonment. All this seems to recall the
Gilbert & Sullivan lines of "Let the punishment fit the crime."

A Public Whipping Without A Whipping Post

The executioner, indeed, may have been busily occupied, at times, because the death penalty could be pronounced not only for murder, but also
for burglary, robbery, polygamy, sacrilege, counterfeiting money, sorcery,
and for selling, giving or delivering "to any Indian, or to any other....

FIRE fire FIRE fire

..... and the ounces of prevention or pounds of cure devised by those of earlier years.

A rope might burn; but this chain "fire-escape," equipped with a spike to anchor it, could enable a trapped person to descend from an upper floor to safety.

1794

Have You Ever Wondered
"What's that Plaque?"

The Sign of the Clasped Hands, so frequently seen on the exterior of houses, means that the home is insured against loss by fire by the Baltimore Equitable Society, the city's oldest corporation.

The Clasped Hands Hang at the Left of the Portico

The famous Carroll Mansion, at Homewood, was first insured under our FIRE POLICY in 1838. In 1866, Mr. Wyman cancelled this policy, and as is always the case, received back in entirety his original payment. In 1903, Johns Hopkins University reinsured the Mansion under the present PERPETUAL POLICY.

Our First Fire Loss

In 1795, William Hawkins insured with us his properties, now the site of the Maryland National Bank Building. The coverage was £1333, 6 shillings, 8 pence. Fire totally destroyed the buildings December 4, 1796 . . . whereupon the Society paid promptly and in full what was its first loss.

"Leathern" buckets were standard equipment for householders and firemen, alike, in the days when running water came from a spring or a pump. A bucket of sand, on each floor, was required in many towns.

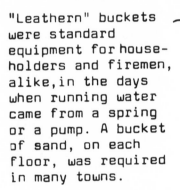

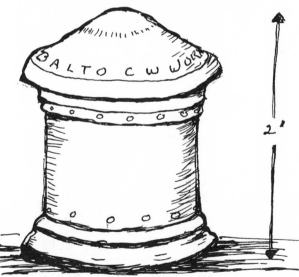

2'

What could be clearer than this cast-iron message looking up from the orange dome-like top of an old Baltimore "fire plug?"

BALTO. C.W. WORKS
20 DOLLARS FINE
TO OPEN THIS PLUG

At the Allegany County Historical Society's Museum, Cumberland, and at Westminister's Carroll County Farm Museum, one may see the original of this ingenious 6-inch-high fire-extinguisher. Made of glass with a sealed top, it could be broken in case of fire, thus releasing a liquid chemical at some spot where it might help to quench the flames.

How People Lived (Cont'd)

enemy of the Province, any gun, pistol, powder, or shot without the knowledge of the Lieutenant-General..." As for the last public whipping in Maryland (in the late 1800's) a difficulty existed because there was no whipping
post in Annapolis. However, this problem was solved by tying the offender
(a Postmaster convicted of tampering with the mails) to one of the handsome
columns supporting the portico of the Maryland State House!

   (Those desiring more detailed information about this subject might con-
   sult "Our Police, - A history of the Baltimore Force, from the First
   Watchman to the Latest Appointee," 1888, edited by de Francais Folsum,
   Baltimore, Md. and also "Crime and Punishment in Early Maryland," by
   Raphael Semmes, 1938, pub. by Johns Hopkins Press, Baltimore).

Police and Fire Protection

   Police protection and fire-fighting were in their infancy until the
1800's. The town watchman, carrying his lantern and wooden rattle, was a
beginning from which we have developed our familiar present-day police
forces--- including fast-moving radio-equipped squad cars. Fire-fighting,
in the early days, was entirely on a volunteer basis. There actually were
occasions when rival fire companies (each claiming to be the first to
arrive and therefore the one to take charge of putting out the fire) began
fighting one another instead of fighting the fire. In some cases, indeed,
the buildings they were supposed to be saving burned to the ground before
the winners of the fist-fights had chased the other firemen home. Nevertheless, these volunteer firemen were mainly the ones who organized the
very first fire insurance companies of America.

   Prosperous 18th-century towns and cities, here and there, were fortunate
enough to own handsome and rather efficient hand-pumper fire engines. One
of these is illustrated on Page 7, bearing the inscription: VICTORY, 1755,
ANNAPOLIS, MD. This particular engine was restored by Museum Services of
Bethesda, Maryland, for the Independent Fire Company of Annapolis, and was
exhibited during the 1966 Annapolis Fine Arts Festival.

   This type is sometimes known as the "Philadelphia" style because it
made its first appearances in Philadelphia between 1750 and 1760. Pumping
handles are located at opposite ends of the engine. Earlier American engines, and those of English manufacture, had pumping handles on opposite
sides.

   Troughs on either side were filled with water. To operate, strong-
muscled firemen grasped the lower and upper wooden handles (often called
"brakes") and pumped them up and down at about 60 strokes a minute. Water
was pulled into each cylinder on the upward stroke, and then forced out
and up into the "condensation chamber" on the downward stroke. After sufficient pressure was built up in the chamber, water was then forced out
through a "play pipe" or nozzle, directed by a fireman standing or kneeling
at the top of the engine. So long as the water supply lasted, this equipment was surprisingly effective. Indeed, a major problem was not its lack
of efficiency "on the job," but, instead, the tendency of men to bruise or
break fingers when they attempted to catch the fast-moving handles.

   Such hand-operated equipment continued in use during the 1820's and
even later. Both then and earlier, however, smaller or less prosperous
communities were obliged to depend upon "bucket brigades"---groups of
volunteers who passed buckets of water from hand to hand.

How People Lived (Cont'd)

The Workman's Wages

The workman's lot was not always entirely happy. Laws, for many years, protected owners and employers rather than wage-earners. As an example: If a builder could not pay everything that he owed, those who had supplied lumber, bricks, and other materials had first claim. After bills for such materials were paid, workmen could collect their wages--- that is, they could collect if the builder still had any money. Laws to protect workers (known as "mechanics' lien laws") did not exist until the mid-1800's. During the 1600's and 1700's, therefore, workmen were frequently paid last of all--- or not at all.

Both farmers and skilled workmen had a reasonably secure position of self-support and community respect in the colonies during the fifty years before the American Revolution. To earn enough, however, some workmen turned from one trade to another. A man who worked as a carpenter during the summer might earn money at night, or at other seasons, as a blacksmith or stone-mason.

The "Upper Crust"

The most fortunate of all were the planters, high government officials, and the "idle rich." They were the colony's "upper crust." Their wives and daughters were able to import much of what they wore--- linens from London, silks and satins from France or Italy, and laces from Belgium. Prosperous men wore costly imported garments for their visits to Annapolis, the capital city, when the General Assembly was in session. At such times the theatrical and racing seasons were in full swing. Buckled shoes, silk stockings, embroidered waistcoats draping almost to the knees, wigs topped by three-cornered hats, and either dress swords or walking sticks-- these were among the adornments of "upper class" men. They travelled in as much comfort and style as the bad condition of the roads would permit. Even so, that difficulty was eliminated whenever it became possible to travel by water. Then they glided gently along in barges, rowed or sailed by liveried servants; and in the larger towns, the ladies might be carried in sedan chairs by their servants.

Upper and Lower Classes

Life had been a struggle, in the 1600's. The mere difficulties of earning a living and of staying alive made it difficult to have a society divided into classes. Very few people had much time for play or for social life. Since nearly everybody worked from twelve to sixteen hours a day (including Saturdays) it was customary for workers to spend an hour or two just "resting," (or reading) before going to bed. By the 18th century, however, it became possible to divide the population into two groups; "upper classes" and "lower classes." It can be said, though, that the outlines of a "middle class" were beginning to show, faintly. This slowly developing "middle class" included some successful small farmers and shopkeepers as well as craftsmen (mentioned previously). These craftsmen, having served "their time" as apprentices, could feel reasonably sure of supporting themselves, and their families, by using their special knowledge and skills, and by working hard. They were helping to change primitive backwoods settlements into thriving centers of culture, art, commerce, and invention. They were creating happier ways of living.

▲▲▲▲▲▲▲▲▲▲▲▲▲▲▲▲▲▲▲▲▲▲▲▲▲▲▲▲▲▲▲▲▲▲▲▲▲▲▲

Chapter 2

A Day In The Life Of Jimmy Randall

It was bitterly cold that Monday morning in January when Jimmy Randall awakened. For a few minutes, he burrowed comfortably among the warm blankets and then he remembered that there was a special reason why he must get up early on this particular morning.

Last night, he remembered, his father had forgotten to bring in firewood and the fire in the big fireplace had gone out, leaving the house cold and sending everyone to bed earlier than usual.

This morning, therefore, it would be his job to start a fire, using flint, steel and tinder. Through his thoughts went the countryside's old saying about the patience needed to start a fire in this way: "If you have good luck, you can get a light in half an hour."

Shivering, Jimmy pulled on his clothing, and wrapped one of the blankets completely around his shoulders, for good measure. For a moment, he looked at the pitcher of water sitting in a washbowl on top the washstand, but quickly decided to postpone washing his face and hands until the house would be warmer. Then, down the squeaking stairs he crept, treading quietly to avoid awakening his mother and father in the big front room, and his sister, Anne, who slept in the middle room. There was no comforting candle to push back the shadows, but he knew the feel of every tread and had not a moment's hesitation.

Downstairs, he lifted the heavy iron bar on the side door and stepped out of doors. Overhead, thousands of frosty bright stars gave just enough light for Jimmy to make out the dim outline of the woodshed. With practiced tread, he felt his way along the path, carrying several armloads of wood back to the house.

Then he was ready for the ordeal which, when successful, would strike a few sparks from his steel and flint into the waiting tinder. As it turned out, this tedious job wasn't necessary. From the kitchen window, Jimmy spied a light in the kitchen of the Goodwin house, their nearest neighbor. Carrying the brass shovel which always hung near the kitchen fireplace, Jimmy slipped out the side door and soon returned, having borrowed some live coals from Mrs. Goodwin's fire.

(As recommended by Benjamin Franklin, many families carried hot coals in a warming-pan <u>with the lid closed</u>, "else scraps of fire may fall into chinks and make no appearance until midnight when, your stairs being in flames,you

A Day In The Life Of Jimmy Randall (Cont'd)

Note: "Jimmy Randall," is a composite character, not an actual person. His day is given to show how a boy might have lived then.

Nearly every home had its own water supply - a well, dug deep into the ground. A rope and a bucket served to bring up cool water.

may be forced - as I was - to leap out of your windows and hazard your necks to avoid being over-roasted.")

Now the flames surged upward as he began to build his fire---shavings and twigs first of all, then larger bits of wood, and finally some dry logs. The water in the big iron kettle had frozen into a solid chunk of ice, but Jimmy hung it on the fire-place crane, knowing that it would eventually give all the family some heartening drinks of hot tea.

It was still dark when Jimmy's mother came down, well muffled against the cold, to prepare for the breakfast of oatmeal, fried ham, tea, and chunks of cold cornbread. By then the kitchen had become a place of cheer,

Coal was scarce; kerosene had not yet been made from petroleum; and electricity (though Franklin and others were making many experiments) was not yet the servant of man. Wood provided warmth <u>twice</u>, someone remarked: First, when you <u>chopped</u> it; and second, when you <u>burned</u> it.

A Day In The Life Of Jimmy Randall (Cont'd)

two candles adding their glow to the gathering flames in the fireplace. Into a small iron pot, near the end of the crane, Jimmy ladled just enough water from the big pot so that his father would have hot water to shave.

Hurrying through breakfast, because school sessions began at half-past eight, Jimmy started off on his walk of nearly two miles to school. On the way, he was joined by Billy Worthington and Harry Dorsey, who studied with him in the sixth grade. Billy was carrying an armload of tobacco, the payment being sent by his parents for their share of the term school expenses.

All subjects, with special emphasis on reading, penmanship and problems of arithmetic, were taught by one teacher, Mr. Dowsley, and all the classes were held in one room. All the scholars were boys. Anne, and the other girls of the town, had their lessons at home. They learned reading, writing, and "ciphering" (arithmetic) at times when they were not being kept busy with kitchen or other household duties.

In the morning, Jimmy's lessons went along slowly and painfully. This was partly because the ink froze on his pen several times, and partly because he spent a great deal of time using his knife to sharpen the writing end of his pen--- a large goose feather. Having used all the paper in his own home-made copy-book, Jimmy was obliged to write out his lessons on several loose sheets, until he could make another copy-book from foolscap paper. Then his mother would carefully sew it into book shape, and Jimmy would rule it by hand, using the tomahawk-shaped leaden plummet which he always had handy, tied to his ruler.

Firewood for the fires, which were kept burning constantly in the school's two fireplaces, was supplied by the parents of the students. The boys took turns, day by day, in feeding the fires with wood and in cleaning up ashes.

Noon-time, which was also lunch-time, brought several special treats. Mr. Dowsley joined a group of boys, at the fireplace, and shared some cider which they heated at the fire until it was piping hot. In anticipation of just this, some of the boys, including Jimmy, had brought some corn, and soon this was popping, snowy-white, from the fire's steady glow. Meanwhile, dozens of sandwiches were being toasted at the fire and one of them, twisting sideways from an improvised skewer, had to be rescued and brushed off after falling among some ashes.

After lunch, Jimmy and a dozen others played ice-skating catchers on a nearby pond. Their cheeks were glowing, and the wintry cold was forgotten

A Day In The Life Of Jimmy Randall (Cont'd)

when Mr. Dowsley came to the school-house door, ringing the bell for the afternoon session.

After school, that day, Jimmy, Billy, and Harry, wandered down toward the river, instead of going directly home. For half an hour, or more, they prospected around looking for traces of a runaway slave for whom a reward of eight Spanish dollars had been offered. But there was no luck for them, though it may have been good luck for the slave who had chosen to run off from his master's "bed and board, and kind treatment."

After supper, in Jimmy's home, candles were not burned for long, because of the expense. All thought of games was put aside until daylight hours, so that the brief period of candle-light could be used for studies. Then came evening prayers, and a few minutes of family singing, with Mr. Randall's bass voice adding volume to the thin clear voices of Anne, and Jimmy, and their mother's soprano.

Finally, with a last look at the kitchen fire and its big slow-burning back-log, Jimmy climbed up to his room, and soon was sound asleep.

Bathrooms, kitchen sinks, and other plumbing do not date back much beyond the late 1800's in American life. Even today, in some rural areas, farm dwellers continue to use seven-piece china sets like the one in Jimmy Randall's room. Besides the wash bowl and pitcher (holding almost a gallon of water) a typical set includes a soap dish and a tooth-brush mug. Also, hiding inside the swinging door of the wooden marble-topped washstand is a china slop-jar (to hold dirty water after washing). Sets of this kind now command high prices in antique shops.

Our word "plumber" comes from the older word, "plumbum"--- another name for lead. In earlier times, a plumber was often called "the plumbum man." No worker deserved either name until he had mastered the difficult art of joining two leaden water pipes by using melted lead. This task was called "wiping a joint." Plumbers of today work faster and better by using light but equally rust-resisting copper tubing. "Wiping a joint," therefore, is forgotten, except in plumbing history; but the word "plumbago" is used, sometimes, to mean graphite.

Chapter   3

Life On The Frontier

Life in the well-settled middle-Atlantic colonies was far different, during the 18th century, from that in pioneer settlements toward the west and north.

Those living east of the mountains (whether in towns or on farms) enjoyed a greater variety of food. They had more conveniences. They also escaped such dangers as attacks by Indians; malaria (then called "the ague") or other dreaded diseases (with no doctor nearer than half-a-day's journey); and crop failures, from drought or insect pests (with no neighbors near at hand, or able to help very much). After a serious injury, an eastern farmer could very likely secure help from a neighbor, or passerby. Beyond the Monocacy River, a man might die from the same sort of injury, simply because no one was near.

The Thick Forest Was Everywhere

Westward and northward, the forest was almost everywhere. Great trees, with inter-twining grapevines and Virginia Creeper, shut out the light. There was plenty of sunlight only along swamps or rivers, and at certain places such as Great Meadows, Pennsylvania, or the cleared fields of an occasional settler. The forest (though it was sometimes a pleasant place to gather berries, nuts, or persimmons) was also a source of many dangers-- whether real or imaginary. Only too often, those living alone became insane, or perhaps "just a bit queer," because of constant worry.

Every woodland was: 1) A dark place of mystery.
                                      2) An enemy, in itself, which would "take over"

Today, people still say "the latch string is out"--- meaning that visitors are welcome. In older days (especially along the western Maryland mountain frontier), when the latch string was dangling <u>outside</u> the door (through the <u>hole, as shown</u>), <u>any passerby, as well as</u> members of the family, could pull the <u>latch</u> up (from outside) and enter the house.

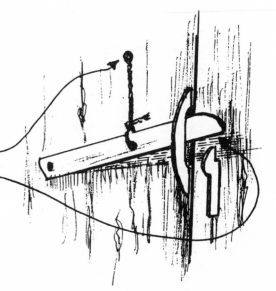

the Pennsylvania Rifle

Although known for years as the "Kentucky Rifle", the celebrated long rifle of muzzle-loading days was developed in Lancaster County, Pa., & built chiefly in the shops of such Pennsylvania gunmakers as the Henrys, John Armstrong, Mathew Roesser, N. Beyer, the Lemans, D. Cooley, Henry Koons, John Moll, the Dreppards, Philip Lefevre, the Zorgers & others...

Early locks were entirely hand-made — down to the smallest Screws, springs & pins...

The barrels were forged from iron bars in charcoal fires, and were rifled on primitive wooden rifling machines...

Stocks were made of native maple, carefully selected for beauty of grain. Many were embellished with intricate carved designs...

Patchboxes, thimbles, butt plates, trigger guards and the various inlays found on the long rifles were fashioned from brass or silver, and were usually decorated with delicate engraving..

A leather hunting bag containing lead balls, a knife, patching material and a horn full of powder usually accompanied the woodsman and his rifle...

Superbly accurate, the Pennsylvania rifle won fame on the frontiers of America — feeding hungry mouths, defending pioneer homes and establishing the freedom of the Colonies.

— C. Stanley Smith

This "picture story" about the Pennsylvania "long rifle" has been reproduced from <u>Historic Pennsylvania Leaflet No.4,</u> through the courtesy of the Pennsylvania Historical and Museum Commission and the Pennsylvania Game Commission.

Life On The Frontier (Cont'd)

> hard-won cornfields and pastures, unless trees and brush were cut down.
>
> 3) A hiding place which might (and often did) contain poisonous snakes; poison ivy; stinging insects; wild animals such as mountain lions; and causes of various mysterious diseases -- in addition to Indian scouts or war parties. Less frequent dangers were forest fires and falling trees.

Some Comparisons Of Daily Life

Along Western and Northern Frontiers

(From the Monocacy to the Youghiogheny and beyond; and from the Potomac to Pennsylvania-- and beyond)

When Indian attacks were a threat, a farmer could not work in his fields without taking great risks. Entire families usually took shelter in a nearby "blockhouse," living there for weeks.

Pioneer farmers were limited, in planting, to those seeds which were already being planted by Indians (such as squash and corn), or others brought in from overseas (such as cabbage, wheat, rye, and turnips). It was necessary to bring these over the mountains by packhorse, or on a man's back.

Clothing was "home made," except for those durable garments worn by the family during its hard journey through the Blue Ridge foothills and misty mountain slopes of Frederick County. Often, a garment outgrown by one child was given to a younger brother or sister.

Hunting and fishing were looked upon, principally, as ways of obtaining food.

It is natural to think of frontiersmen as erect, healthy, and even athletic. However, because so much of their work required bending over in one cramped position, they became stiff and "stooped." Both men and women grew old "before their time." The dates carved on old tombstones show that a great many frontier women "died young." Furthermore, poor health sometimes was caused by a limited variety of food (too starchy or too fatty).

On Eastern and Southern Farms

A farmer could plant when he chose, weather permitting.

Crops of many kinds could be planted. Seeds of new varieties could be bought upon arrival in ships from other countries.

Prosperous families could wear fine imported silk, woolen, linen, and other fabrics (stuffs), and could buy expensive jewelry.

Hunting and fishing were, often, for sport.

Life On The Frontier (Cont'd)

Along Western And Northern Frontiers

Hospitality was an "unwritten law" of the wilderness country. Anyone who came to the door was offered food (if there was any), and shelter (even if it meant sleeping on the floor). Strangers were welcome because they brought news.

Until about 1730, those white men who travelled through the mountain regions were traders,hunters, and trappers. They brought back crude maps showing Indian trails and rivers, and all sorts of information such as the locations of salt springs and clay deposits (for making bricks). Since they were constantly moving about, they had no reason to take (or buy) land from the Indians, and to build fences around it. Land was still like the ocean: Everyone could travel on it, in any direction. Much of the trouble with Indians came, later, when they began to feel that their hunting grounds were being taken from them by settlers (whether by bargaining for beads, or just by force).

Living alone,or with few neighbors, frontier families were forced to work hard and to be self-reliant. There is all the more reason, therefore, to respect the courage, initiative and skill of Jonathan Hager, who was resolute in opening Western Maryland to settlers. Those who would like to gather "on-the-spot" impressions of his "House-Fort and Fur-Trade Post" (1739-40),should visit the faithfully-restored and authentically furnished Hager House (not far from downtown Hagerstown). There, they may "relive 18th-century day-to-day history on the spot." Numerous coins, as well as great quantities of glass, pottery, and metal everyday objects were unearthed quite near the foundation when restoration work was begun in 1953. It would be a mistake to leave without seeing these, in the nearby Hager Museum.

Few women continued to be widows for very long. They were anxious to marry again, for protection, and to guard

On Eastern And Southern Farms

There were more inns as the population grew. It became customary for strangers to stop at an inn, and pay for their food and lodging.

More and more, those in or near towns such as Chestertown,Oxford, Baltimore, and Annapolis learned the advantages of working together in a common cause, for cultural and civic improvements (such as fire-fighting, schools, churches, and markets).

Life On The Frontier (Cont'd)

against starvation.

Courage, and willingness to help either
a neighbor or a passerby-- these were
among the frontiersman's good qualities.
Yet he was likely to be opinionated, re-
sentful of law or its authority, re-
fusing to pay taxes.

Most of those journeying to "the Forks of the Ohio" (French: Fort Du-
quesne; British: Fort Pitt; now Pittsburgh) went by way of Western Maryland,
usually turning northward at Wills Creek (now Cumberland). Braddock's ill-
fated expedition began in this way.

Thomas Cresap And Others

Our respect for Thomas Cresap's courage, and skill in dealing with the
Indians, increases as we consider that for many years, his trading-post and
inn at Oldtown (nine or ten miles south of present-day Cumberland) was sur-
rounded by the wilderness. He succeeded so well in winning the respect and
friendship of the Indians that they called him "Big Spoon" (since he was
generous in sharing food with them). Because of their liking for him, there
were many times when he was able to bring white men and red men together,
and settle arguments. He must have looked quite different, in earlier years,
to settlers from Southern Pennsylvania whom he tried to drive away."Thomas
Cresap...appeared with three hundred men in arms... with Drums and Trumpets
to Strike Terror into the Inhabitants..."

In 1732 (as the Maryland government enviously watched a stream of German
settlers flowing from Southern Pennsylvania to settle in the fertile Shenandoah Valley of Virginia), Lord Baltimore invited other Germans to settle
in Maryland, saying:

"Wee being desirous to Increase the Number of Honest People within our
Province of Maryland... doe Assure all such that they shall be as well Se-
cured in their Liberty and Property in Maryland as any of his Majesty's Subjects in any part of the British Plantations in America."

Sad to relate,however, most of those who settled in and around such
towns as Middletown (1740), Lewistown and Myerstown (1745) and Mechanics-
town (1751) were terror-stricken when they began receiving such reports as
this after Braddock's defeat (1755):

"On our march... we found John Meyer's house in flames, and nine or ten
head of large cattle killed.About 3½ miles farther up the road we found a
man killed and scalped,with one arm cut off and several arrows sticking in
him..."

(A report from Conococheague,printed in March 11,1756 Maryland Gazette).
NOTE: Conococheague, long a westernmost settlement (between present-day
Williamsport and Clearspring) gradually disappeared - principally be-
cause nearby Hagerstown steadily grew and prospered.

Chapter 4

Entertainment And Sports

Not to Maryland, but to Pennsylvania, belongs the honor of organizing America's first symphony orchestra. This was founded in 1741 by the Moravians who settled at what is now Bethlehem. By 1748, their little orchestra had two first violins, two second violins, two violas, one 'cello, one double-bass, two flutes, two trumpets, and two French horns. It was playing symphonies by the Austrian composer, Haydn, within a year or two after he had composed them.

An Opera Orchestra

Maryland, however, was not content with occasional "tinkling on the harpsichord" and dance music. An orchestra was formed for giving opera in Annapolis, during June of 1752, when Gay's "The Beggar's Opera" had a number of performances.

Franklin's "Musical Glasses"

Near Annapolis, about 1765, Benjamin Franklin gave a concert on the Harmonica (also called the "Armonica" or "Glassychord") which he had recently invented (See illustration). Franklin, who showed great talent in playing the harp and the guitar, based his invention upon the "musical glasses" which had been popular in Europe a few years earlier. For the Harmonica, he made saucer-like glass discs of different sizes, and these were fastened and balanced on a spindle. These glass discs could be rotated by foot action, using a pedal somewhat like that of a spinning-wheel. Since the lower portions of the glass bowls (or discs) were immersed in water, they would produce tones when the fingers of a player were touched to their revolving top edges.

A description of music played by the Harmonica is in the diary kept by Philip Vickers Fithian while he was teaching the children of a Virginia planter, Robert Carter: "Evening, Mr. Carter spent in playing on the Harmonica; It is the first time I have heard the instrument. The music is charming. He play'd 'Water Parted from the Sea!' The notes are clear and inexpressibly Soft; they swell, and are inexpressibly grand; and either it is because the sounds are new, and therefore please me, or it is the most captivating Instrument I have ever heard. The sounds very much resemble the human voice, and in my opinion they far exceed the swelling Organ..."

BENJAMIN FRANKLIN'S HARMONICA (Armonica)
(Foot pedal missing)

Entertainment And Sports (Cont'd)

Dancing

No doubt about it, Annapolis was a center of entertainment and social life in Maryland, until Baltimore slowly but steadily developed as a rival, following the American Revolution. Taken from a diary of the times, here is a description of evening gaiety: "Wine, lemon punch, Toddy, Cider, Porter... About seven, the Ladies and Gentlemen began to dance in the Ball Room-first Minuets one round; Second, Giggs;... and last of all, Country Dances; tho they struck several Marches occasionally. The music was a French horn and two violins. The Ladies were dressed Gay and splendid, & when dancing, their Skirts and Brocades rustled and trailed behind them..."

Dancing was so popular with both young and old that few concerts were given which were not <u>followed</u> by dancing. Larger cities had their Assembly Rooms, built principally to house the balls and other activities (including concerts) supervised by the leading dancing master.

George Washington's Visits To Annapolis

It was to Annapolis that the wealthy planters came not only for visits, but also to attend the theatre, balls, the races, and sessions of the General Assembly. Some idea of the social life and entertainment enjoyed by George Washington, during one of his many trips from Mount Vernon to the capital city of Maryland, is shown in his diary for September, 1771:

"Sept. 21 Set out with Mr. Wonneley for the Annapolis Races. Dined at Mr. William Digges, and lodged at Mr. Ignatius Digges.

22 Dined at Mr. Sam Galloway's, and lodged with Mr. Boucher in Annapolis.

23 Dined with Mr. Lloyd Dulany, and spent the evening at the Coffee House.

24 Dined with the Govr., and went to the play and ball afterwards.

25 Dined at Dr. Stewards, and went to the play and ball afterwards.

26 Dined with Mr. Ridout, and went to the play after it.

27 Dined at Mr. Carroll's, and went to the ball.

28 Dined at Mr. Boucher's, and went from thence to the play, and afterwards to the Coffee House.

29 Dined with Major Jenifer, and supped at Dan'l Dulany, Esqs.

30 Left Annapolis, and dined and supped with Mr. Sam'l Galloway.

Oct. 1 Dined at Upper Marlborough, and reached home in the afternoon."

Circus Performances

Early in the 1700's, the circus was already rather well known as a form of public amusement, though performances were not as fine as those we see today. It probably had its beginnings in America when lone trappers came

Entertainment And Sports (Cont'd)

out of the woods leading tame bears, and had them do their tricks--- afterwards passing the hat among the bystanders for a collection. To Philadelphia, however, goes the distinction of presenting the first American circus troupe of which we have a printed record (in 1724).

Innkeepers welcomed men who owned bears or other animals, because such "animal acts" attracted many more customers to the inns. Quite frequently, sailors appeared with pet monkeys which could do various tricks. Other animals were brought to this country from Africa, South America, the West Indies, or Europe, and placed on exhibit. In Boston, during 1716, a lion was shown to the public for an admission charge, and both a camel and a polar bear were exhibited there, later.(The advertisement for this said: "The like never before has been seen in America!") After 1724, old newspaper files show that there were also circus performances in which clowns and acrobats took part.

Later,(1814) "Peale's Baltimore Museum" on Holliday Street mentioned in its descriptive folder: "Its first floor was occupied by mounted specimens of birds and animals, and a surprising variety of live animals as well!"

Theatrical Performances

More or less typical of performances given by travelling theatrical companies in Baltimore, Chestertown, Annapolis, and Upper Marlboro are those described in this advertisement which appeared during June, 1752, in the Maryland Gazette:

"By permission of his honour the President, at the New Theatre,in Annapolis, by the company of Comedians, on Monday next, being the 6th of this instant July, will be performed:

T H E   B U S Y   B O D Y

likewise a Farce, called

T H E   L Y I N G   V A L E T

to begin precisely at 7 o'clock

Tickets to be had at the printing office

No persons to be admitted behind the Scenes.

N.B.   As the Company have now got their Hands, Cloaths, etc.,
compleat, they now confirm their Resolution of going to
Upper Marlborough,as soon as ever Encouragement fails here."

Performances of Shakespeare's "The Merchant of Venice" also were given. The company announced that it had "Scenes, Cloaths and Decorations... all entirely new, extremely rich... excell'd by none in Beauty and Elegance, so that the Ladies and Gentlemen may depend on being entertain'd in as polite a manner as at the Theatres in London."

Social Life In Annapolis

No sooner were the important crops harvested than the more prominent

Entertainment And Sports (Cont'd)

planters (and some who were not) started out to enjoy social life in Annapolis. Here, the Governor, other government leaders, other planters and
their families, and leading citizens of the city were all equally ready
for some days and nights of pleasant living. Afternoons and nights of gay-
ety, dancing, horse-races, card-playing, and other social amusements always marked "public times" (when courts were in session and other govern-
mental activities were scheduled). There were times, too, when such important visitors as the Marquis de Lafayette, Count Rochambeau, or General
Braddock, together with their staffs of officers wearing splendid uniforms,
were in town--- ripe and ready for entertainment.

Horse Races

George Washington's diary gives frequent evidence of his fondness for
watching (and placing bets on) horse races. In this, he had a multitude
of 18th-century company, as shown by old newspaper mentions of "Jockey
Clubs." There were important racing seasons at various points, just as today, but at quite different locations:

Upper Marlborough	Annapolis
Port Tobacco	Leonard-Town
Frederick	Bladensburg

Visits By Ship Captains

At home, the planters and their families looked forward to the arrival
of ships from England. These would tie up at the wharves of large plantations, ready to unload merchandise ordered months previously from business
firms in England. They were always very interesting occasions. The captains and officers brought all the latest news from London or the West
Indies, along with welcome cargoes of tools, wines, and "stuffs," or rum,
sugar, and molasses. It became an enjoyable matter of playing host and hos-
tess to walking, talking "newspapers"--- loaded heavily with all the standard gossip from overseas. In an exchange of courtesies, there was usually
a dinner "on board" before the ship's officers and crew would tear themselves away, and sail on to the next center of trade and hospitality.

Free Food And Lodging For The Traveler

Outside the towns, it was customary for each family to provide food and
lodging, free of charge, for all highway travelers who asked for it, whether
they were strangers, close friends, or acquaintances. Such hospitality was
given without question by everyone, rich or poor, because there were not

Entertainment And Sports (Cont'd)

many inns; travel was slow, at best; and distances between towns were great. Travelers depended upon it, especially on long trips. Two great pioneer American botanists, John Bartram and his son William, made use of such hospitality when they travelled as far south as Florida (from Philadelphia) to gather specimens of plant material. Indeed, few travelers stayed overnight at inns, unless these happened to be of the better type found in larger towns (where free hospitality for all was not the usual rule, anyway).

Hospitality Becomes A Burden

Hospitality, for all travelers who might come to the door, began to be a heavy expense by the mid-1700's--- especially for those living near main roads. Thomas Jefferson actually built another house to avoid the numerous expensive and time-wasting visitors who came to "Monticello" (his beautiful mountain-top home near Charlottesville, Virginia). Jefferson's second home, located in an inland part of Fairfax County, was called "Ravensworth." It was his custom to spend many months of each year there.

Too much Drinking Was Fashionable

An interesting remark about the drinking habits of the times was made about 1789, by one of the best-known planters and government leaders: "I can perceive a great reformation in my countrymen in this respect: that they are less given to intoxication; that it is no longer fashionable for a man to force his guests to drink, and to make it an honour to send them home drunk; that you hear no longer the taverns resounding with those noisy parties formerly so frequent... and that the distinction of classes begins to disappear."

The Courthouse - A Gathering Place

Just as one might suppose, the days when court was in session were the occasions for playing games, for sociable gatherings at the town square, and for equally sociable lounging outside the courthouse. Here, or nearby, men often played such out-of-doors games as ninepins (bowling). The game of ninepins became so noisy and disturbing that it was banned in some sections of colonial America. A way around this difficulty was found by adding one more pin to the game. Thus, Americans play tenpins, today, though much the same form of bowling continues as ninepins, overseas.

Fishing As a Sport

Maryland because of its many rivers, creeks, and inlets has an almost unbelievably long tidewater shoreline. Consequently, fishing--- both

Entertainment And Sports (Cont'd)

saltwater and freshwater--- has always been a leading sport since the early days of the Calverts.

Said Captain John Smith, who explored the Chesapeake Bay (1608) long before Leonard Calvert arrived with the "Ark" and the "Dove":

"... abundance of fish, lying so thicke with their heads above the water, as for want of nets (our barge driving amongst them) we attempted to catch them with a frying pan; but we found it a bad instrument to catch fish with; neither better fish, more plentyous nor more variety for small fish, had any one of us seene in any place so swimming in the water, but they are not to be caught with frying pans."

(Continued next page)

Queen Anne Folding Card Table (once owned by Thomas Jefferson, and now in the Maryland Historical Society's collection).

According to local legend, an early resident of Charles County not only had fifty couples of fox-hounds but actually "kept a poker game going continuously here for forty years!" The fine old house which was the home of this pleasure-loving gentleman is Mt. Republican (built in 1792, with brick walls 2½ feet thick). The house is frequently opened to visitors during house and garden tours.

Very likely, he and the other card-players used a "gaming table" like that sketched above (also used for such other card games as "loo.") Antique collectors, today, know that the four oval saucer-like depressions (at each player's left) were used to hold money and called "guinea pockets."

A candlestick could be placed to give light at each of the four corners. A fifth leg could be swung out to support a hinged leaf which, when folded back, reduced the size of the table top and gave a flat surface for other use.

Entertainment And Sports (Cont'd)

Hunting And Other Sports

Rich man and poor man, slave and free man - all spent many hours in hunting. This, like fishing, had the additional advantage of bringing another supply of food to the family kitchen. Bear hunting and fox hunting were popular.

Both hunting and fishing were a way of life for some families who lived on the edge of the wilderness. The many dangers and risks are told in the book entitled: "Forty-Four Years Of The Life Of A Hunter- Meshach Browning." This son of a soldier who had escaped from Braddock's battle, was a match for the rugged life in the Allegany Mountain region. Roughly written down in his own words, Browning gives a clear picture of hunting scenes. From the best estimate he could make, he killed:

> "Eighteen Hundred to Two Thousand Deer
> Three To Four Hundred Bears
> About Fifty Panthers and Catamounts (quite as ferocious,
>   and not much less in size than
>   the panther)
> Scores of wolves and wildcats."

Both hunting and warfare must have been slow work, at times. "Firelock" and "matchlock" guns were in general use until about 1640 when "flintlock" weapons began coming into general use. Each of these was fired by means of a hard brown flint fastened to the hammer. The flint (when the hammer was released by pulling the trigger) struck sparks by hitting against a piece of iron. The sparks set fire to a little gunpowder in the "priming pan" which then exploded the larger amount of gunpowder in the gun barrel. Flintlocks (both rifles and pistols) continued in use until about 1840, when "percussion cap" weapons became popular. (See illustration, page 17).

Other Leisurely Activities

Horse-racing, dancing, gambling, card-playing, and even cock-fighting occupied other leisure moments of gentlemen in colonial times. There were many other indoor and outdoor diversions. Included were games such as battledore and shuttlecock, chess, backgammon, billiards and message cards. Although neither playing cards nor dice have survived, archaeologists have found relics in Williamsburg of billiards, dominoes and a game called loo.

Advertisements From The "Maryland Gazette"

(1782) "Thos. Graham has billiard table with balls, tacks, etc. for sale.."
(1783) "Cribbage Boards and Backgammon tables for sale by Shaw and
        Chisholm at the house of John Shaw near Stadt House."

Social Clubs

Finally, there were the social clubs which buzzed with activity. Many of these were exclusively for men, but one and all they were dedicated to pleasure. Life was not exactly dull in colonial Maryland,--even if moving pictures, television, and sports cars were not there to brighten the scene.

Chapter 5

Friendly Enemies
(Indians, Pirates and Smugglers)

Maryland was fortunate in being spared those wars with the Indians which caused so much bloodshed in most of the colonies. There were several reasons for this, one of the chief ones being the generally peaceful disposition of most Indian tribes in Maryland.

Furthermore, until about 1675, the colonists managed to keep on reasonably good terms with the warlike Susquehannocks who lived along the Susquehanna River Valley but who often came southward into Maryland. These Susquehannocks, belonging to the large family of tribes known as Iroquois, claimed that their hunting grounds reached southward to the Patuxent River, on the western shore, and to the Choptank River, on the other side of the Chesapeake Bay. Since most of this same territory was claimed either by the Nanticokes (near what is now Vienna, on the Eastern Shore) or by the Piscataways (living between the Patuxent and the Potomac) there were frequent wars among the Indians, themselves. See map at the beginning of this book.

"Coexistence"--- Seventeenth-Century Style

Even before the Maryland colonists arrived in 1634, their future relationship with the Indians was favored by geography; by the nature of the Indians settled there as well as by their contacts, in turn, with neighboring Indian "nations"; and also by the locations of Indian villages and hunting areas. Tribes living along the Potomac and Patuxent (including the Yaocomicos, Anacostins and Piscataways) had reason to fear the warlike Susquehannocks. These always claimed hunting rights toward the south. Thus, some purely Indian skirmishes and wars were likely to result when the Susquehannocks migrated from their usual Susquehanna River villages. Naturally, Indians of Southern Maryland were happy to join the St. Mary's City settlers in defense alliances. The colonists, quite as naturally, were glad to have as many Indians as possible on their side. Before many years passed, the Susquehannocks, too, were willing to arrange a mutual defense pact. They, it appears, feared Indian attacks from the north--- by the Senecas. Meanwhile, the Bay and its many rivers provided Maryland's new foreign-born citizens with reasonably safe means of travel--- by boat.

Common among grievances of settlers were such matters as damage done to carefully-planted vegetable patches by live-stock which the Indians allowed to roam at large. From time to time, also, one or two Indians couldn't resist convenient opportunities of stealing some interesting pieces of English-made hardware or colorful clothing. The Indians, for their part, felt that individual colonists "took advantage" in land deals or in paying them much less than their furs were really worth.

Everything considered, there was comparatively little bloodshed. Partly because of treaties (and a show of patience in hearing grievances) early Maryland was spared the large-scale warfare of most sister colonies.

Friendly Enemies (Cont'd)

"Coexistence," in the twentieth century, is a modern dilemma of international life faced by the nations of the world. "Coexistence," in colonial America, was really an armed truce between those friendly enemies (or warlike friends)-- the colonists and the Indians. Punctuated by negotiations, treaties, and treaty violations this truce was stirred up, now and then, by France. She sought to use the Shawnees and Delawares on her side, against the Iroquois Five Nations (later Six), either allied with the British or neutral. Neither side had any real reason to love the other side. Yet each side usually considered it wise to go through outward forms of friendship, especially because some possible advantages, and dangers, were mutual.

By the late 1670's, the Susquehannocks (although leaving behind them a trail of burning barns and murdered farmers) had left Maryland, to live in Southern Virginia. The Nanticokes, complaining of unfair treatment moved from Maryland's Eastern shore, in the mid-1700's, to north-central Pennsylvania (near the present-day city of Nanticoke). There, they placed themselves under the protection ("on the cradle-board") of the powerful Six Nations. Most of the more-peaceful Piscataways had already drifted southward to live in mountain regions of Virginia. Thus, long before the redcoats replaced the redskins as a principal threat, the estimated number of Maryland Indians had decreased from between 5,000 and 7,000 to not more than a few hundred. Maryland's Indian period had ended.

Lessons Learned From The Indians

Meanwhile, however, the settlers had been learning valuable lessons from their Indian neighbors concerning the ways of wind and weather, woodcraft, fishing, hunting, and agriculture.

From them, they received seeds of Indian corn (which the Indians called "maize"), squash, pumpkins, gourds, sunflowers, or tobacco, and they learned how to plant and grow them. They also learned the Indians' method of mixing dried corn with lye, to remove the tough skin around the kernels. In this way, they could make hominy, by long cooking over a "slow" fire. Deer fat (or suet) could be used for many cooking purposes, they learned, and "corn pone" could be cooked on hot stones, (or a metal griddle), after the corn had been ground by a mortar and pestle. (See illustration).

Seasons And Crops

The Indians of Maryland, it has been said, divided the year into five seasons: "1) The budding of spring; 2) The earing of corn, or roasting-ear time; 3 Summer or highest sun; 4) Corn-gathering, or fall of the leaf; and 5) Winter, which they called cohonk."

Indian Corn And Its Many Uses

Indian corn was considered one of the most important crops by Indians and colonists alike. If planted in April, it furnished roasting-ears for

Friendly Enemies (Cont'd)

use as a green vegetable in early summer. When gathered later, the ears of corn provided grain for corn meal or hominy to be eaten in autumn, winter or spring. The grain, furthermore, provided nourishing food for livestock and fowls. In addition, the blades (or corn leaves) could be used as food for cattle. The shucks (coverings of the ears of corn) furnished stuffing for mattresses, the bottoms for chairs, and even the stalks could be used to make shelters for cattle and bedding in the cattle sheds.

Some of the salves, oils, and ointments made by the red men from different roots and berries were added to the settlers' medicine chests, and so were other medicines made from various kinds of bark, roots, and leaves.

Tobacco

Quite early, "smoking the pipe of peace" also led the settlers to adopt the Indian custom of smoking, and to plant and cultivate tobacco. This became Maryland's biggest "money-crop"- actually worth <u>more</u> than "its weight in gold."

Indians "shooed" birds away from their corn and other crops, like this, instead of saving time and trouble by using "scare crows!"

Government

Although they could not read or write as we do, Indians had well-organized governments. Usually (as in Maryland), four, five or six tribes were loosely organized as a sort of confederacy under one emperor, or (in Indian language) <u>Tayac</u>. In each tribe, there was usually a War Chief, known to them (and to Captain John Smith) as the <u>Werowance</u>, or <u>Sachem</u>. However, his decisions apparently were limited to certain activities. Others were decided by a council of peace (its members called <u>Wisoes</u>). Shawnee tribes, it is said, sometimes had <u>female</u> chiefs. Their principal mission,

Continued next page

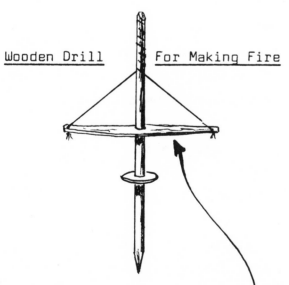

<u>Wooden Drill</u>   <u>For Making Fire</u>

Pressing the movable <u>cross bar</u> down (and then letting it come up again) made the point of the drill revolve rapidly. When pressed against soft dry wood, with some thin shavings close at hand, the friction would eventually cause the wood to become quite hot; to char; to smoke; and to produce some sparks which could be "fanned" (with careful nursing) into a small blaze.

▲▲▲

Friendly Enemies (Cont'd)

apparently, was that of attempting to persuade a War Chief from deciding to make war. The War Chief, himself, was a veteran of at least four war parties, bringing home both scalps and a record of successful battle.

Different tribes and different Indian nations, naturally, had somewhat different customs. A Shawnee brave once remarked that, by examining an encampment, he could name the Indian nation to which its occupants belonged. He explained that Shawnees (living in Western Maryland for many years) would have a kettle suspended from a horizontal beam. This would rest upon two forked sticks placed vertically in the ground. Indians of other nations would perhaps use the cross-wise beam in different ways, or suspend the kettle from a single stick extending <u>across</u> the fire.

(Since there were so many other interesting differences of custom among Indians, those seeking more detailed information may well consult Pages 18-24 of The WPA guidebook entitled: <u>Maryland- A Guide To The Old Line State</u>"; and the authoritative paper-bound volume: <u>Indians in Pennsylvania</u> (giving information about Maryland as well as Pennsylvania red men). Written by Dr. Paul A.W. Wallace, it is available from <u>The Pennsylvania Historical and Museum Commission, Harrisburg</u>).

Money And Trading

Ordinarily, Indians depended upon trading to exchange what they had for other things they wanted. They were so successful in "swapping" that scientists of today have found, along the <u>Atlantic</u> coast, Indian possessions which could have originated nowhere else except along <u>Pacific</u> shores.

Still, even in their primitive uncomplicated lives, they felt that they needed what we would call "a medium of exchange"--- money. Indian money consisted of polished bits of clam or oyster shell (sometimes ground into the shape of cylinders, pierced through their centers, and strung together like beads). This was known as <u>wampum</u>. The name comes from an Indian word, <u>wampumpeak</u>, meaning "strings of white shell beads." The thick purple-black wampum (often called <u>peak</u>) was two or three times more valuable than the plain white variety (known as <u>roanoke</u>).

Besides using it as money, most Indians also made belts from their best <u>wampum</u>. To some extent, these helped them to overcome their lack of well-organized written languages (other than "picture writing"). To them, these <u>wampum</u> belts represented their tribal customs and honor. For ceremonial occasions, a tribe's "wise men" would exhibit them, especially to their young "braves," to inform or remind them concerning great events of each tribe's history.

"Wampum was sacred," writes that noted Indian authority, Dr. Paul A.W. Wallace. "For a speaker in council to hold a <u>wampum</u> belt in his hand was like a white man's laying his hand on the Bible and taking the oath.

Friendly Enemies (Cont'd)

(' What Indians say with hand upon the wampum belt is true', said Chief William Dewaserage Loft... of the Mohawks). In public debate, strings or belts of wampum served to refresh the memory... The touch and sight of the belts helped both speaker and audience to follow the argument... White wampum was a symbol of peace; black wampum, of grief or death... In historic times, wampum belts usually had designs inwoven in dark beads on white ground to indicate the terms of a treaty or the substance of a message..."

(Note: The famous Penn Wampum Belt, to be seen at the Historical Society of Pennsylvania, in Philadelphia, contains about 3,000 beads arranged in eighteen rows. Traditions say that it records the treaty held late in 1682 under the Shackamaxon Elm, in Philadelphia. This promised peace between the people of Delaware Chief Tamanend (or Tammany) and William Penn, "as long as grass grows and water runs." It shows an Indian and a white man, with clasped hands. Voltaire wrote that this treaty was "the only one not sworn to, and never broken."

Houses

The houses of Indian villages were always located near a river or stream (to make sure of having a water supply). These houses (or huts) were built by driving boughs of trees into the ground- forming two opposite rows,with the large ends down, and roughly sharpened to points. These boughs were then pulled together at the top, and firmly tied. (See illustration below).

Such huts were naturally quite smoky and drafty, when fires were built in them - for heating and cooking - during cold weather. Nevertheless, several families (with a total of from six to two dozen men, women and children) lived in each! Some people think that all Indians lived in tents or "teepees." This was true only of certain tribes (mainly in the West), who liked to carry their houses on their backs or on their ponies. Artifacts found at the restored Jonathan Hager House, Hagerstown, show that the Shawnees, living in Western Maryland,built rather substantial wooden houses.

Continued Next Page

Tidewater Maryland and Virginia Indians made and used this kind of house. It was a hut covered with brush or hides, and had a "roll up" door (as shown). There was an opening, at the top, to let smoke escape. Those who visit Jamestown, Virginia, can see, there, a hut of this kind, in the replica Indian village.

~~~~~~

Friendly Enemies (Cont'd)

Log Canoe Making

Indian canoes of Maryland, for the most part, were made by hollowing out a
log of the proper size. Since the work of chopping was hard, Indians <u>burned</u>
out a great deal of wood, chipping away later with hand tools. Perhaps some
canoes were made in Maryland by fastening bark of trees or animal skins
over a wooden frame. These, however, were more frequently found farther
north. During the 1800's, the Chesapeake Bay log canoe, propelled by sails,
became a popular type of workboat. It originated as an outcome of the
Indian "dugout" log canoe; but its construction required as many as four
to seven logs. Around 1880, more than 6,000 sailing log canoes were in use,
on the Chesapeake. Now, there are only a few.

Continued From Page 33

Games

   Gambling was a favorite amusement of all the Indians, and the men played
a number of different games using a ball. In one of these, they struck the
ball with a bat, or stick. Another ball game originated by North American
Indians is popular today under the name of lacrosse.

Hunting

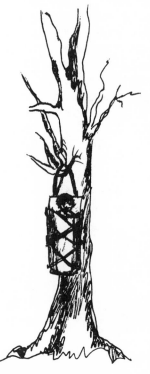

When it came to hunting deer, the Indians were well
equipped to act as teachers. They would trap considerable numbers of deer by building a circle of fire, four
or five miles in diameter, which they would gradually
narrow. Or, as a variation of this, they would scare the
deer out onto a point of land, so that hunters in canoes
could cut off any retreat by water.

During the hunting season, as many as several hundred
braves and squaws would band together and leave their
villages unoccupied for several weeks at a time. When
hunting alone, for deer, an Indian would cover himself
with a deer skin "showing horns, ears, eyes, and mouth.
Thus shrouding his body in skinne by stalking, he
approacheth the Deere, creeping on the ground from one
tree to another."

Some Customs

"To harden their babies," one writer has commented,
"the mothers took them on the coldest mornings to the
waters and plunged them in for a bath, and moreover,
they so painted and anointed them that their skins became tanned and toughened in such a manner that, after
a year or two, no weather would hurt them."

Friendly Enemies (Cont'd)

Though usually brave in battle, they actually had many fears. They thought that "evil spirits" caused thunder, lightning, floods, and bad weather conditions.

Towels to dry their bodies, were unknown. After getting wet, they merely shook themselves. To make knives and hatchets they slowly and patiently ground pieces of stone or shell to a sharp edge. Oyster shells, also sharpened to an edge, were used as razors for shaving.

The Indians had very simple means of measuring time according to phases of the moon, the changes from day to night, the growth of plants, the flight of birds, and so on.

Lessons The Indians Learned

Trading skins and furs of otter, mink, deer and beaver, for such articles as fish hooks, knives and axes, metal cooking pots and trinkets, went on for many years. At the same time, the Indians adopted many of the colonists' worst habits, such as drunkenness. So well did the Indians learn, indeed, that many of their own accomplishments were neglected. We are told that the Piscataways, within fifty years after Maryland was settled, had almost forgotten their once-prized art of making bows and arrows!

A Few Among Many Popular Misunderstandings
About Friendly Enemies Of Colonial Days

Customary Belief: Indians and other wilderness travellers found their way
          by locating the direction of north. They could determine this either
          by observing the stars (especially the Big Dipper and the Pole Star),
          or by noticing that moss grows thickest on the north sides of trees.

Fact: In those early days, the woods were usually so thick overhead that
          stars could not be seen except in fleeting glimpses. Observation of
          thick-growing moss on tree-trunks might be helpful when the travel-
          ler was lost. But it was not his business to get lost. Besides,
          there were many times when he was really in a hurry, to deliver warn-
          ings, dispatches, or perishable food. Experienced forest travellers
          followed the Indian paths. The real difficulty, however, was to make
          a choice because, with few exceptions, more than one path existed.
          Paths made by hunters or fishermen, for instance, could be time-
          wasting because of their many side-excursions. Therefore the veteran
          frontiersman's real gift lay in recognizing (either by experience,
          or from markers left by others) the trail best suited to his purpose.

Customary Belief: Indians and colonists, alike, used trails already made by
          animals.

Fact: Wild animals, such as deer, having completely different interests
          from those of human beings, wandered about a great deal. Indians, it
          is believed, made their own paths, using animal trails only when
          they had found the one safe convenient way over or around some
          natural obstacle (such as a mountain or waterfall).

Customary Belief: Colonists and trappers, when travelling through the for-
          est, hoped that they would not meet any Indians.

Fact: On the contrary, it would have been either a short or a most unusual
          journey if no small groups of Indians were encountered. The forest,
          at times, was a rather busy place. Indians and colonists, alike, con-
          sidered it polite to exchange greetings, including the latest news

▲▲▲

Friendly Enemies (Cont'd)

or gossip. If the Indians had killed some game, recently, they might even offer a haunch of venison. In most Indian villages of the East, women kept a pot of stew over a "slow" fire, ready to offer as a gesture of hospitality to any peaceful traveller who might arrive.

Customary Belief: Tight-fitting clothing of Indians and frontier settlers, so often shown on TV or in motion-pictures, can educate us concerning their clothing customs.

Fact: Early travellers, explorers, peddlers, and hunters invariably needed loose hunting shirts into which they could tuck extra items of food or equipment. A strong belt around the waist kept all this loose material handy, and protected from damp weather. Likewise, plain leather shirts or pants were not entirely popular--- because they were cold in winter, and felt "clammy" when wet. Animal hides having fur on the outside were favored because they would "shed water." Clothing having fur on the inside, or lined with wool, was preferred during cold months, since it prevented body heat from escaping.

Customary Belief: Travellers either slept in tents, or in the open, with no protection.

Fact: It is true that the great maker of Indian treaties, Conrad Weiser, carried a hammock during his travels of later years. Count Zinzendorf, noted Moravian pioneer leader, preferred to take a large tent, when travelling with pack-horses. These, however, were not only "luxuries;" they were quite unusual. Just as in the Southwest of today, a traveller might think nothing of sleeping under the open sky, with only a smoldering fire and a loaded rifle for company. Yet every ten or twelve miles, along important Indian trails, Indians had built cabins or sheds which anyone could use. Sometimes, a traveller seeking such shelter, in wet weather, would find that the last occupant had left some food, as a gift to the next person. Old maps and journals mention many of these better-known shelters by name, such as "Cock Eye's Cabin" or "Warrior's Spring."

Customary Belief: Hitler's "lightning war" (blitzkrieg) and Japan's "Pearl Harbor" attack started a modern fashion of "undeclared war."

Fact: Actually, elements of surprise attack, undeclared war, and terrorism (including torture of captives) were favored by North American Indians, in general. History tells us, however, that these had all been used by various nations and ethnic groups before discovery of America--- and that the conquering Spaniards and Portuguese used them against Indians of Latin-America.

Customary Belief: Indian men compelled women of the tribe to perform "manual labor" such as farming and gardening, in addition to their more customary duties as housewives and mothers.

Fact: This work was a generally-accepted and well-understood custom in their "division of labor." Everyone had duties to perform, including children. Women, being nearly always at home (and "closer to the land") accepted, without question, their agricultural tasks--- more in the nature of gardening than farming. The "braves" (strong young warriors) felt that their games and apparent play were actually preparation for the dangerous and difficult arts of hunting, survival in the wilderness, and warfare. One commentator has pointed out that Indians were horrified to learn that white men ill-treated Indian women and sold their children into slavery. He has also stated that Indians "showed respect for the person of woman, even in time of war." To this, he added that most women and children captives, and many of the men, instead of being put to death, were adopted into Indian families and treated with kindness. Another writer has spoken of deep love between Indian husbands and wives, though never publicly shown. An Indian husband, he mentions, travelled a hundred miles and back again, to obtain some food for his sick wife. He traded his horse for "as much corn as filled the crown of his hat" and, carrying his saddle, returned to her, on foot.

Pirates ---- And Smugglers

Looking back into mid-Atlantic colonial history, it would be easy for us to make the mistake of regarding Indians as the greatest year-round colonial danger. Actually, for many who lived along tidewater areas of the Eastern and Western shores, pirates were more feared--- and less likely to give warning of their intentions.

Pirates in mid-Atlantic waters are mentioned only briefly, or not at all, in many books or articles about the colonial period. Quite frequently, there is mention of Blackbeard (off the Carolina-Georgia coasts) and Captain Kidd (from New York harbor southward). Yet Blackbeard was no stranger to the Chesapeake Bay and its Maryland-Virginia capes (Cape Charles and Cape Henry in particular).

Francis Nicholson, as Governor of Maryland (1694-99) and as Governor of Virginia (beginning in 1699) frequently asked British authorities to send more armed ships, to protect shipping against piracy. On one dramatic occasion (in spring of 1700) he sailed aboard H.M.S. Shoreham and personally supervised pursuit and capture of a large ship, La Paix, in the vicinity of Lynhaven Bay.

As late as 1722, Benjamin Franklin's brother, James, made a few sharp-edged comments in the New England Courant, concerning the absence of any British men-of-war in the Chesapeake Bay region. He pointed out, "the bold pirate, George Lowther" was actively engaged there. James wrote and published, August 6, 1722: "On Sunday the 22nd (July) arrived a small sloop (at Philadelphia), Jonathan Swain, Master, from Cape May, by whom we have Advice that a Pyrate Brigantine and Sloop have been cruising on and off our Capes for above Three Weeks. They were both seen, on Thursday last... not fearing disturbances from the Men-of-War who, by dear experience, we know, love Trading better than Fighting."

Meanwhile, more than a few Maryland merchants and shipyards were willing to "wink the other eye" when doing business with pirate captains and their

Friendly Enemies (Cont'd)

crew members. Skillington's shipyard, on the Tred Avon, was a 17th and 18th-century pirate haven. Tour books of the <u>Maryland House and Garden Pilgrimage</u> tell the story of a notorious pirate named Combes, or Coomes. It appears that many acres of Talbot County land were given to him in exchange for his promise to give up a bloody but profitable career and retire there (along Island Creek, off the Little Choptank).

"Hole-in-the-Wall," near Easton, was a pre-Revolutionary retail outlet for smuggled goods.

Ferocious Blackbeard was killed by a brave Virginian, in 1718, but it was not until the late 1700's that the <u>Frigate Constellation</u> swept nearby saltwater free of pirate ships.

Smugglers were less dangerous but there were more of them. Any neighbor, in those days, could have been doing some smuggling in his spare time. Secret tunnels leading from some old houses toward salt-water may have been built for this purpose, quite as much as for escape from enemy attack.

The fine art of bringing in British merchandise without paying taxes to Britain became more and more popular as the "Spirit of 1776" grew. There were many reasons. For one thing, British Trade and Navigation Acts, increasingly severe, made it difficult to do business with any country except England. Meanwhile, all concerned resented the increasing taxes on goods coming <u>from</u> England. Finally, smuggling was not too difficult along the Chesapeake's many winding and lonely tributaries, especially for those who had learned the ways of wind, wave, and cutlass aboard privateers.

Some Devices Of Smugglers

Among principal "short cuts" and ways of avoiding capture and punishment, smugglers had in mind:

A) The transfer of merchandise, otherwise taxable, from one ship to another, at sea.

B) Loading or unloading by night, at lonely piers.

C) The use of misleading (or entirely false) manifests (lists of cargo items)

▲▲

Friendly Enemies (Cont'd)

> D) The use of purposely incorrect labels on barrels and crates.
>
> E) Sending non-taxable goods to Holland or France, and then bringing back "luxury" items such as silks, tea, or wines, without first entering (as British law directed) a British port (where taxes would be collected).
>
> F) Bringing in rum or molasses from <u>foreign</u> ports of the West Indies, but labelling and reporting them as imports from the <u>British</u> West Indies.
>
> (One report of the times states: "Several Scotch merchants in Pennsylvania drive a continual trade into their country, and from thence carry the tobacco of Maryland and Virginia to Surinam and Curacao in bread casks covered with flour at each end...." Also, in 1705, Governor Seymour, of Maryland, complained about the difficulty of keeping shipping statistics adding "it is impossible for all the officers in the world to know what is shipt or unshipt, because of smuggling.")

▲▲▲▲▲▲▲▲

For Additional Information About Pirates, Smuggling, And Indians

Some few books which the authors have found especially helpful (and dependable) are listed near the end of this book, (under the three headings given above) in a section headed: LIST OF USEFUL BOOKS.

There are many others of equal or even greater value. Therefore, this section, and this chapter, may well be regarded merely as starting-points for additional interesting journeys through forests or across ocean horizons of two exciting centuries.

If the reader already has some of this feeling he may understand that a sympathetic attitude is often more important than gathering a bristling array of dates and other statistics. Therefore, reading (or re-reading) could well include Robert Louis Stevenson's "Treasure Island" and Howard Pyle's well-illustrated stories about pirates (half-fact and half-fiction). Fiction about Indians, on the other hand, could well be avoided, entirely. An informative book, nonfiction, is: <u>Shipwrecks, Skin Divers, and Sunken Gold</u>, by Dave Horner, illustrated; index. Dodd Mead, NYC.

######

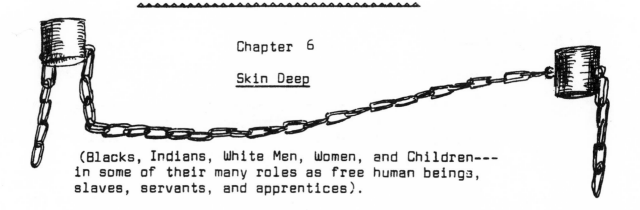

Chapter 6

Skin Deep

(Blacks, Indians, White Men, Women, and Children---
in some of their many roles as free human beings,
slaves, servants, and apprentices).

Slavery was an everyday way of life for many in colonial Maryland, in colonial America and, indeed, throughout the world at that time and earlier. Such bondage could last for years (as mentioned earlier, under "indentured servants"); or it could be for life--- unless escape brought deliverance.

Especially sad chapters of slavery were provided by kidnapping. In England, for instance, many children and drunkards were kidnapped (or "shanghaied"). Most, very likely, were shipped as slaves to North America, South and Central America, or the West Indies. If they were lucky, they served for only four to seven years and then were given freedom. In all too many cases, their slavery ended only when they died, or were too crippled to work.

Indian Children Were Kidnapped-- To Be Slaves

North American Indian children, too, were kidnapped, usually to serve as slaves. Escape was difficult, especially when they were shipped to faraway areas, such as New England. This became one more grudge--- and an important one--- held by Indians against colonists and traders as a whole.

Verrazano, when he landed along Maryland's ocean coast (apparently not far from present Snow Hill), saw nothing wrong in capturing a few stray Indian children and some trustingly curious adults. He captured and took with him all that were handy. Then, completing his well-known cruise up the coast to discover present New York harbor, he exhibited them in Europe as living proof of his great discoveries. John Cabot did the same when he made his notable explorations for England along the Newfoundland coast, and elsewhere (c. 1497).

Columbus Suggested Slavery For Indians

The greatness of Christopher Columbus was diminished, somewhat, when the noted American historian, Samuel Eliot Morison wrote his book, Admiral of the Ocean Sea. This reports a recommendation to the Spanish monarchs, Ferdinand and Isabella, made soon after Columbus had discovered some able-bodied Indians,

Skin Deep (Cont'd)

together with San Salvador and other islands. The Italian navigator out-
lined the possibilities of gaining wealth, easily, by using these newly-
made friends and neighbors as slaves. (As history knows so well, Spanish
<u>conquistadors</u> began taking not only gold, silver, and jewels, but also
all the healthy Indians who failed to hide from them). It seems equally
apparent that Blacks were imported to Latin American regions (such as
Cuba, Puerto Rico, and Mexico) only after the Indian slave population had
been reduced by hard work, bad treatment, and--- especially--- diseases
brought in from Europe.

Slavery--- An Ancient Practice

Thus we see that in those days (and on back through the crowding centuries) <u>anyone</u> could be a slave--- no matter what the skin color, age, sex,
race, or nationality might be. The very word, "slave," is derived from
"slav," ethnologists tell us (apparently because so many of slavic descent
have been slaves).

Quite likely, we Americans immediately think of blacks when we think
of slaves. The <u>two</u> often have been <u>one</u>, in our history. Yet, when we read
far back and far afield in world history, it appears that other racial
groups have been enslaved in even greater numbers. The <u>Odyssey</u>, and such
famous volumes of fiction-history as <u>Ben Hur</u> and <u>The Last Days Of Pompeii</u>
give us additional viewpoints concerning this endlessly ancient custom---
this demonstration of "man's inhumanity to man."

A Roman Citizen Who Owned Over 4,000 Slaves

From other sources, we learn that one "noble Roman," when he died during the reign of Augustus, left more than 4,000 slaves to his heirs. When
we close our eyes to glimpse the appearance of Roman and Greek galleys, or
of <u>Antony</u> and <u>Cleopatra's</u> warships--- truth will compel us to see, as
well, long rows of chained sweating men. These would be the galley slaves.
They would be beaten if they did not pull (or pull hard <u>enough</u>) on the
long sweeping oars. They would be likely to die by drowning if their
galley were defeated in battle.

Gladiators--- And Debtors Who Became Slaves

Numerous muscular slaves of ancient Rome were compelled to fight as
gladiators before huge audiences, living dangerously and perhaps briefly.
Besides captives taken in war, Roman slaves included debtors who could not
pay. In any case, such slaves of Rome (and other Mediterranean countries)
had no political rights; they depended for good treatment entirely upon
the good nature of their owners; and their masters could use whippings,
branding, and execution to obtain obedience.

America's First Black Slaves--Brought By Portuguese

Oddly enough, Portuguese (rather than Spaniards) brought the first shipment of Black slaves to the New World, landing them in 1503 at Santo Domingo.
Portuguese were also the first who made a business of hunting and taking

Skin Deep (Cont'd)

slaves in the African interior. Then, and later, African chieftains and other natives were the ones who, for payment in money or rum, delivered other natives into captivity at the hands of European ship captains or traders. These were usually captured at night when they ran to escape from devouring flames as their villages burned. Today, though officially pro- hibited, slave-holding still continues, it is reported, in some Portuguese and Mohammedan regions.

It was in Europe that the first slaves from Africa were sold. Not until 1619, mainly by accident, was the first shipload of these slaves landed at Jamestown, Virginia.

Maryland--- Home Of Free Blacks As Well As Slaves

Equally strange, at first glance, is the fact that comparatively few Blacks were in Maryland before the latter portion of the 17th century. This can be understood better when it is recognized that they were actively sought as labor when tobacco was seen as Maryland's great "money crop."Just when black slaves were brought into the Province is not really known. There is a record of bargaining by Governor Leonard Calvert with a shipmaster, in 1642, for delivery of 13 black slaves at St. Mary's City (Maryland Archives, IV, 189).

Not always realized, today, is the fact that more than a few Blacks of colonial Maryland were _free_ men and women. Benjamin Banneker's father, and his mother's parents, were born in Africa. In earlier life, his father was a slave; but, after marriage, his wife purchased his freedom. Later, the couple bought a farm of about 100 acres, paying 7,000 pounds of tobacco for it.

Blacks Come From Many Different Ethnic Stocks

Another misunderstanding is the belief that all blacks have come from the same ethnic stock.

So great have been the differences of origin that, when herded unwill- ingly together in slave ships, these unfortunate people often were unable to understand one another's languages. Brothers in misery, many were strangers in language communication. An ethnic authority, Mr. Amram Scheinfeld, has suggested an easy way to realize that _more_ genetic differ- ences existed among groups of blacks coming from different regions, in slavery days, than could be found among _white_ immigrants. He has suggested observing such differences today, at one spot, by noticing the great con- trasts in appearance and speech of African delegates at the United Nations sessions.

Skin Deep (Cont'd)

Legalized Forced Labor-- By Whites As Well As Blacks

White convicts and indentured servants, arriving from England in ship after ship, provided a large share of the 17th-century work force in Maryland and Virginia. To their "forced labor" was added the work of apprentices who worked while learning a trade. There was a great rush to "get rich quick" by planting tobacco, toward the late 1600s, that brought in more and more slaves.

A Johnson From Sweden Becomes A "Free Man"

Offering sharp contrast is a recent statement by former Secretary of Agriculture Orville Freeman. During one of those fascinating and informative television conversations with lovely Deena Clark (Channel 4, Washington, D.C.) he remarked that his grandfather's name was Johnson. But, added Secretary Freeman, his ancestor changed his last name from Johnson to Freeman. Why? Because he had left Sweden and settled in America to become a "free man"--- and, besides, Johnson has always been a very common Swedish name.

Maryland's Slave Population Decreases, After 1750

From about 1750 on, in Maryland, two ways of thinking gained increasing strength. Eventually, they also gained widespread popularity. The first one was inevitable. It recognized that tobacco, year after year, robbed the soil of its fertility. Therefore, the tobacco crops decreased in value, size, and quality, year after year. Poor quality tobacco and reductions in crop yields meant something more than reduced income, for tobacco farmers. Plantation owners and small farmers, alike, felt unable to afford their former expense in feeding, housing, and clothing slaves. At this point, Maryland's slave population began to decrease. Partly, this resulted from the sale of no-longer-needed slaves "down South."

JUNE 16, 1763
TEN POUNDS REWARD
Ran away from the Subscriber living near Soldier's Delight in Baltimore County, on the 9th of June last, a Servant Man, named David Wickenden. Is fond of liquor, much given to chewing tobacco, and is a notorious Rogue.
Alexander Wells

Remarks Of A French Traveler

......."Pass into Maryland and Virginia (from Pennsylvania) and........ you are in another world; you find not there those cultivated plains, those neat country-houses, barns well distributed, and numerous herds of cattle, fat and vigorous. No: every thing in Maryland and Virginia wears the print of slavery; a starved soil, bad cultivation, houses falling to ruin, cattle small and few...... in a word, you see real misery, and apparent luxury, insulting each other."

"They begin to perceive, even in the Southern States, that, to nourish

‸‸

<u>Skin Deep</u> (Cont'd)

a slave ill, is a mistaken economy; and that money employed in their pur-
chase, does not render its interest. It is perhaps more owing to this con-
sideration than to humanity that you see free labour introduced in a part
of Virginia, in that part bordered by the beautiful river *Shenadore. In
travelling here you will think yourself in Pennsylvania..."

(During the year 1788, M. Brissot de Warville wrote some sharply-etched
opinions and descriptions as he travelled along the Atlantic coast to
visit General George Washington, at Mount Vernon, Virginia.His remarks,
including those quoted above, are in an old book, largely based upon
his letters and diary entries, entitled <u>New Travels in the United
States of America</u>. Returning to his native France, he was sent to the
guillotine some years later, during the "Reign of Terror.")

<u>"The Age Of Reason"</u>--- Also An Age Of Ethics

A second way of thinking, with little direct relation to the economics
mentioned above, began to have great power and permanent effect. The "Age
of Reason" was beginning. Some slave-owners, as well as those opposing
Britain's "taxation without representation," might have been willing to
call it, as well, an "Age of Ethics."

New ideas had been expressed by such philosophers as John Locke.Since
then, some have even said that he might be called "father of America's
Declaration of Independence." The rights of man became subjects of daily
conversation. If white colonists were rebellious because Britain's King
and Parliament were ignoring their liberty, how could they, in turn, jus-
tify depriving other human beings of <u>every</u> freedom, through slavery?
Freedom to choose one's work and living place--- freedom to move about
without hindrance; to vote; to express one's opinions--- all these, and
more, were forbidden for slaves. The lot of an indentured servant was
little better, at times.

<u>Changing Slavery Into Freedom</u>

Here, then, lies an explanation for the actions of men such as Maryland's Johns Hopkins and William Paca in giving freedom to their slaves.
It was not easy to do this. An able-bodied slave was worth anywhere from
500 to 2,000 dollars. But men were beginning to take the longer view. Many
were saying, and seeing, that freedom is "doing anything that I want to do,
<u>provided it does not interfere with the rights of others</u>." More and more,
men were recognizing the hard fact that liberty is not mere license, and
that true freedom can hardly coexist, for long, with legal bondage and
forced labor.

The wine of freedom, once tasted, was intoxicating. The American Revolution, followed by the French Revolution and others, were only outward
evidences of man's new attitudes. Indentured servants ceased to be everyday people whom one met every day and in almost every way.

* Shenandoah River

Skin Deep (Cont'd)

The Maryland General Assembly had ordered a tax of 10 shillings on every black slave brought into Maryland. This was increased several times until, in 1716, the tax was 40 shillings. So far, however, such taxes were mainly for the purposes of raising revenue. The tax, however, was raised dramatically to 500 pounds, in 1780--- obviously so high as "virtually to prohibit the trade." This was done, says Mr. L. Magruder Passano in his old but excellent History of Maryland, "because the people had begun to think that there were already more than enough slaves in the State, and because the feeling that slavery was wrong was beginning to gain ground." Three years later, in 1783, Maryland passed an Act for-bidding altogether any further "introduction of slaves."

Earlier, the trend toward freedom (and toward a willingness to fight for it) was shown by the fact that several thousand or more blacks fought in the Continental Army.

George Mason--- A Profile In Courage, And Ethics

A great war of brother against brother was still to be fought in Amer-ica (1861-65), but it would sweep away all legal forced labor that re-mained in America. Nevertheless, many of its deeds and thoughts would look back to those "free-thinkers" of the later 1700's--- and especially to George Mason, across the Potomac, at Gunston Hall, in Virginia. It was he who attended the Constitutional Convention of 1787 in Philadelphia but who refused to endorse the much-admired Federal Constitution it drafted. His main reason? It failed to outlaw slavery, and (until amended some years later, effective December 15, 1791) it did not include its now-familiar Bill of Rights.

######

Chapter 7

Artists And Craftsmen

For the purpose of earning a living, it was not enough for a man to be one of the finest silversmiths in all America. Artists and craftsmen almost invariably were obliged to develop other ways of adding to their earnings. By operating a ferry or a tavern--- and sometimes both--- craftsmen managed to make both ends meet. In the long lulls between ferry-boating or serving drinks, the artist evidently had plenty of time to work at his latest creations.

Silversmiths

Among silversmiths, such outstanding men as William Faris and John Inch added to their incomes by acting as tavern-keepers. Faris, in addition, was a watchmaker and clockmaker, a cabinetmaker, portrait painter, and dentist. Usually, he spent some of his time in making mirrors. Besides all this, he sold tickets for the theatre whenever a "company of comedians" or other strolling players came to town.

John Shaw And Charles Willson Peale

John Shaw, the gifted Annapolis cabinetmaker, was apparently glad to have the work of making coffins. Charles Willson Peale, for instance, spent only part of his working time as a portrait painter. Among his early activities, he served for a time as a school teacher, on the Eastern Shore

(Cont'd Page 48)

Contrary to what many people believe today, not many bricks were brought across the Atlantic Ocean in sailing vessels. This mistake has often been made because early records mention "English brick"

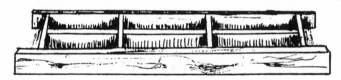

Hand-made bricks were shaped by pressing clay into a wooden mold and then baking them until hard.

In building a house, bricks were laid in "Flemish" bond (like this), in "English" bond, and in other patterns.

or "Flemish brick," meaning the way of laying the brick- and not the place where it was made. Actually, it was not difficult to make bricks in most parts of Maryland, because clay was plentiful.

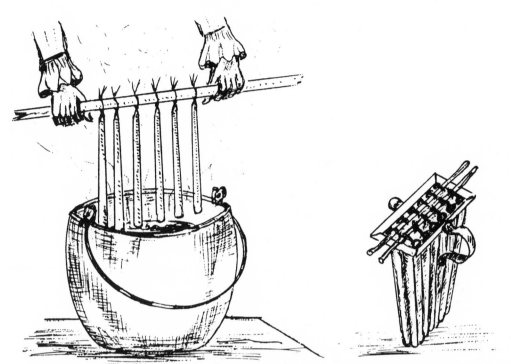

(Left) Candles were made by dipping the cotton wicks into hot wax or tallow, and (Right) by pouring the wax into a mold. By using the mold method, more candles could be made at one time.

The work of making soap, or apple butter, was often done out-of-doors, over an open fire.

△△△△△△△△△△△△△△△△△△△△△△△△△△△△△△△△△△△△

Artists And Craftsmen (Cont'd from Page 46)

of Maryland. During his later and more active years of painting, on the Western Shore, he also was occupied in making and repairing harness and clocks, stuffing birds, and in extracting teeth or making dental plates.

Hand-made Articles

Surprisingly large numbers and quantities of things were hand-made (see Hand Made and "Store Boughten," at the end of this chapter). Balls used in children's games were made of yarn from an old stocking, (or filled with feathers) covered with leather. (Rubber, of course, had not yet come into use).

Old newspapers tell us about some of the painstaking "hand work." For instance, an advertisement in the Maryland Gazette, January 31, 1760 informs readers that:

> "Henry Crouch, Carver from London, now living in Annapolis,
> makes any sort of Carv'd Work for Houses and Ships."

The same paper printed this notice in its January 6, 1774 issue:

> "Joseph Horatio Anderson - coach & herald painter: & varnisher
> to their Majesties & the royal family, proposeth to carry on
> all the various branches of coach & herald painting. Also
> painting in fresco... decorated ceilings for halls, vestibules
> & saloons, either in festoons or fruits, flowers, figures....
> Carved ornaments... in the neatest manner as well as house
> painting..."

Candles were dipped one at a time, into a pot filled with melted wax. (See Page 47). As the level of the wax dropped lower and lower, the candles would touch the bottom of the pot but their tops would not be covered by wax. This produced a "taper shape" which, to this day, is the mark of a hand-made candle. Candles made by pouring wax into molds also had a "taper shape."

Some Articles Used Then - But Not Now

Among hand-made articles much in demand then, but seldom, if ever, used today are:

        Pewter plates; Candle lamps, with reflector shields;
        Clocks operated by weights; Fire Backs (ornamented
        cast-iron plates, used to protect the back wall of a
        fireplace from the heat and ashes of a hot wood fire);
        Ice tongs; Foot Warmers; Irons with detachable handles
        (for ironing clothes); Weighted devices for turning
        Fireplace Spits; Watchmen's Rattles; Fireside Copper
        Kettles; Chairs having a back and sides to give pro-
        tection from drafts--- to mention a few. Some of these
        are considered so attractive, today, that copies of
        them are made and then sold in gift shops. Specimens
        of the original ones (which some people call "antiques")
        may be seen at various museums including the Maryland

The exact age of the cloth doll shown in this drawing (dating from the 1800's) is not known, but it is quite old so far as dolls, in general, are concerned. Instead of throwing the doll away when a new generation was born, a new face was embroidered each time. The fact that there are four faces on this doll (each on top the other) gives some idea of the approximate age. The doll's dress is taffeta (now almost in shreds), and has five petticoats.

Artists And Craftsmen (Cont'd)

Historical Society, 201 W. Monument Street, Baltimore; the
Julia A. Purnell Museum, Snow Hill, and in many colonial homes.

The pace of all such work was somewhat slow. Because there was plenty
of time, even the simple everyday objects were ornamented. It was well before the day of mass production. Consequently, each piece of furniture,
each silver teaspoon, was looked upon as an individual challenge. Craftsmen were so proud of doing fine work that they usually marked their initials, names, or special designs on the things they made. It was a time
when an artist had the time to be an artist, and when great care was given
to "finishing touches." To this loving care we can give thanks, today, for
the many masterpieces handed down by 18th-century workers.

Linens And Woolens, From England--or Somerset County

"... We have little or no Woollen or Linnen manufactures... except
what is done in Somersett County over the Bay, because we are yearly
supplied from England with necessaries..."
(A remark made in 1698 by the Reverend Hugh Jones)

At about that time, Governor Francis Nicholson, commented: "Somerset
County in this province (into which, about ten or eleven years past,
came 600 or 700 of ye Scotch-Irish from Ireland) doth alreddy wellnigh
cloath yourselves and others..."

England, as a fixed policy, always wanted its American colonies to ship
raw materials (to England, and nowhere else), though buying finished goods
made in England, perhaps from the selfsame materials. Despite all this, it
appears that the English Wool Act of 1699 did not hinder Somerset County's
industrious Scotch-Irish carders, spinners, dyers, and weavers. No doubt,
their products were considered "domestic"in nature, because they were used
there, mostly, or nearby. (Incidentally, the spinning-wheel they used was
made possible by that great 15th-16th-century genius, Leonardo da Vinci. He
did not invent the spinning principle, itself, but he did improve upon the
original hand-operated spindle, and other mechanism).

Powder Horns And Drinking Cups Made Of Horn

Some readers may be surprised to learn that there were buffalo herds in
Western Maryland until near the end of the 18th century. This has been con-
firmed in various ways, especially by finding hand-carved gunpowder flasks
made from buffalo horns (as well as from cow horns). In each case, the
large open end was plugged securely, so that none of the precious explosive
would seep out. Then the tip was cut off. This formed a pouring-spout,which
was equipped with a tight-fitting cap, or stopper. (See Page 17, lower
(Continued on Page 54)

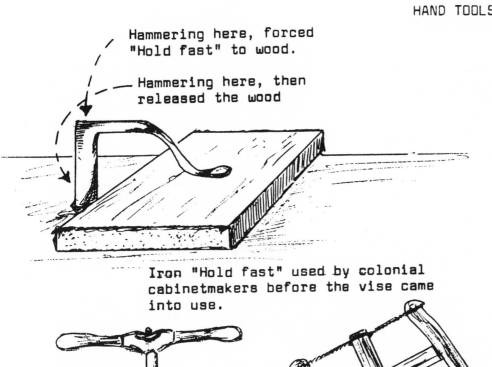

Hammering here, forced
"Hold fast" to wood.

Hammering here, then
released the wood

Iron "Hold fast" used by colonial
cabinetmakers before the vise came
into use.

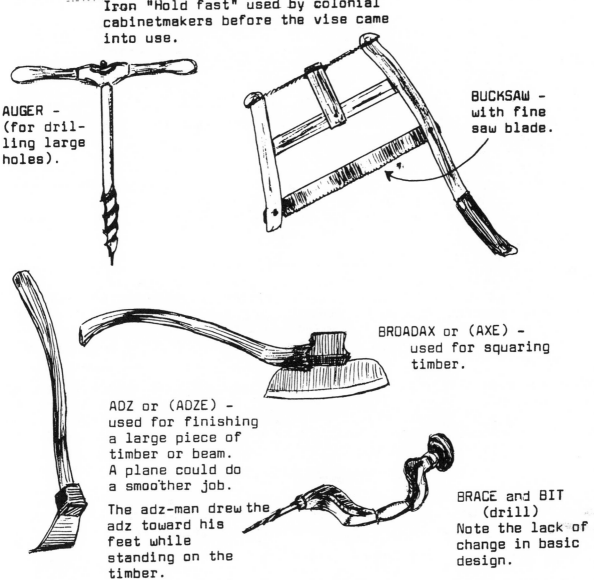

AUGER -
(for dril-
ling large
holes).

BUCKSAW -
with fine
saw blade.

BROADAX or (AXE) -
used for squaring
timber.

ADZ or (ADZE) -
used for finishing
a large piece of
timber or beam.
A plane could do
a smoother job.

The adz-man drew the
adz toward his
feet while
standing on the
timber.

BRACE and BIT
(drill)
Note the lack of
change in basic
design.

Hallmarks of Colonial Artistry

(Silversmiths, Goldsmiths, And Watchmakers)

A silversmith, goldsmith, and watchmaker, of colonial Maryland, could be, and often was (as with Pooh-Bah and his many titles), one and the same person. In any event, he usually "signed" his work by means of hallmarks, stamped or punched into each spoon, bowl, vase, ladle, or other piece. As shown on the opposite page, such hallmarks often gave initials or names, occasionally coupled with picture-symbols.

Hallmarking has been called "a shorthand system which has worked perfectly for almost 600 years." From its earlier years of use, first in England and then in America as well, it has had great value in:

> A) Furnishing consumer protection (see below)
> B) Identifying the maker
> C) Identifying the period (and even the year)
> D) Identifying the country of origin

An Assay Determines The Amount Of Silver

Consumer protection would be mainly concerned with an "assay mark," indicating the percentage of pure silver used. Silver and gold, in their pure forms, are so soft that they are "unworkable." A spoon made of pure silver, in ordinary household use, would be quickly bent out of shape. Usually, the word "sterling" means 92.5% silver, the remainder being some "base" metal, such as copper, to give strength. The amount of each is an important bit of knowledge to any buyer since he "doesn't want to pay a silver price when he's getting copper."

Sterling, the "Easterlings," and Stars

The word "sterling," according to some accounts, is derived from an older English word, "Easterlings." An Easterling, originally, was a craftsman of German descent, living in the east, who did silver work for King John. Others have thought that the word comes from "steorra" (meaning "star" in Old English)--- "steorling" having been a name for a Norman silver penny which had a star in its design.

After 1814, Baltimore silversmiths originated and used a marking system of their own, often using the word "sterling" (as an assay mark to certify that the item is 92.5% pure silver). English smiths, however, have avoided using the word itself on their work but have certified the same degree of purity, since 1719, by using the figure of a lion with one foot raised.

Cabinetmakers And Painters

These, too, usually "signed" their work. Painters, such as Maryland's Charles Willson (or Wilson) Peale have often placed their names, or initials, toward the lower right-hand corners of their pictures.

Famous "old master" instrument makers (such as those of the Guarnerius family, in Cremona, Italy) could not very well display their names or initials on polished wood exteriors of their violins. But they usually found a way of placing some markings inside. In like manner, such a noted Maryland cabinetmaker as John Shaw, of Annapolis, customarily marked his desks, sideboards, and other pieces (perhaps inside a drawer, or under a table top).

Artists And Craftsmen (Cont'd)

Marks Of Some Maryland Silversmiths

The artistry of Charles Faris (second son of another colonial Annapolis silversmith, William Faris) has been recognized by the Metropolitan Museum of Art. In its collection are three of his pieces: a coffee pot; sugar urn; and a creamer. He was born in 1764, at Annapolis, but died there of yellow fever, at the age of 36. Today, advances in medicine have made such diseases rare. We may wonder about the additional beauties this worker in metals could have given us to admire--- if yellow fever had passed him by.

A little later, talented Jeremiah Hughes also worked at this craft in Annapolis, using an equally unusual hallmark (shown here). He was born in Baltimore, 1783.

To understand this marking, we must know that people of colonial America used the letter "I" to serve instead of letter "J." The marking, it is thought, was used by three different 18th-century Maryland silversmiths: James Chalmers, Sr.; John Chalmers; and James Chalmers, Jr. Of these three, John, in 1783, actually minted coins (though not with official approval) in Annapolis. These included a shilling, sixpense, and threepence (using his own original designs). His silver shillings, today, are "collector's items," and priced accordingly.

In somewhat similar fashion, John Inch, a watchmaker and silversmith of Annapolis (1720-62) used this marking on a silver bowl. It was offered as a prize, May 4, 1743, at "the Annapolis Races." Very likely it was America's <u>first</u> horse-racing trophy. Later, his widow, Jane, also used the same mark.

An advertisement in the Maryland Gazette, 1763:

FRANCIS SANDERSON, Copper-Smith, from Lancaster has Settled his Business in Frederick-Town,...where he intends to supply the Public with all Sorts of COPPER-WORK, such as STILLS, BREWING-KETTLES, FISH and WASH-KETTLES, TEA-KETTLES, SAUCE-PANS, and other Things too tedious to mention. N.B. He will give a good Price for all Sorts of Old BRASS, COPPER, PEWTER, and LEAD.

In 1765, Thomas Sparrow, goldsmith, advertised that he could furnish: Tureens, breadbaskets, knee buckles, barometers, doctors' instruments of all sorts and "stone motto rings, with 1, 2, or 3 Doors to lock, for secret Names, and to contain Hair, (such as was never made before)."

Artists And Craftsmen (Cont'd from Page 50)

left-hand corner). When we see these powder horns in museums, we will notice that their carved decorations show not only stars, flowers, forts,
maps, and animals, but also--- in some instances--- initials and names of
their owners. Carved drinking glasses, also made from buffalo horn, may be
seen in the dining room of the Hager House, Hagerstown, Maryland.

Some Old Ideas Which Still Could Be Used-- In Time Of Need

In our twentieth century we may still see, for ourselves, how some of
the old "handicrafts" have been kept alive. (Some could offer practical
present-day help if included in"survival kits" for use after making forced
landings in jungle areas, "where the pavement ends").

As September turns into "October's bright blue weather," The Springs
Folk Festival (situated between Grantsville, Maryland and Springs, Pennsylvania) includes such activities for men as:

> Hollowing out wooden troughs with an adze; splitting shingle
> blocks with froe and mallet; shaving tool handles or shingles,
> using a shaving knife and a "shaving horse" (German: Schnitzel-
> bank): hewing beams with a broad axe; splitting rails, using
> wedges and an axe; threshing grain, by using hand flails; the
> use of horses on a treadmill, to operate mechanical equipment;
> boring wooden water pipes; blacksmithing; and shoeing horses
> or mules.

> Other activities, for women, include: carding wool,(followed by
> the work of spinning and weaving); rug making; quilting; candle-
> making; and--- last but far from least--- cooking and bread-
> baking.

> Demonstrations of still other activities by men or women, some-
> times working together in teams, include: Boiling maple syrup
> to make Spotza, and making apple butter--- both over open wood
> fires; making apple cider; bee-keeping; knitting; basket-
> weaving and chair-seat weaving; pottery "throwing," using a
> potter's wheel; metal work; making dolls from corn husks; and
> wood carving.

Portrait Painters

Some of the more active portrait painters, who traveled from town to
town, carried with them nearly-completed pictures on which clothing and
backgrounds were already painted. Then anyone who ordered a portrait
could choose from among the previously-painted costumes and backgrounds.
After that--- Presto!--- the face and hands were painted in, and the
portrait was finished in record-breaking time! Evidently some of these
painters--- including such a Maryland notable as John Hesselius---

Artists And Craftsmen (Cont'd)

used "short cuts" in production methods a century or more before the
makers of silver and furniture. Drawing hands, ears, and feet, furthermore, were difficult problems for some of the less gifted or insuffi-
ciently trained colonial painters. Quite a number, in fact, were house
painters who gradually branched out into such sidelines as portrait and
landscape painting.

Among noted artists who painted portraits in Maryland, were Charles
Willson Peale, Sully, and John Hesselius. Such artists usually found that
they were also in demand to do pictures of houses, favorite dogs, or race
horses.

Clocks, Watches, And Sundials

"Keeping Time, Time, Time

In a sort of Runic rhyme.."

Our respect for watchmakers (whether colonial or modern) increases very
much when we know that some watchscrews are only four to ten-thousandths
of an inch in diameter. (A dozen or more could fit over the period at the
end of this sentence). Because such watch parts are so small and delicate,
they will pick up moisture from a human hand. Fortunate, therefore, is the
watch craftsman who has what German-speaking Swiss jewelers call a
trockene hand (a dry hand).

Two Unusual Clocks

Two colonial-made clocks in the 1700s were amazing. One
was the clock made by that black genius, Benjamin Banneker (c. 1734-1806),
of Baltimore and Howard Counties. (Although he had never seen a clock, he
constructed one based upon his own drawings. These showed the arrangement
of parts in a watch he owned). The other clock (made in Bucks County,
Pennsylvania, about 1769) was the work of Joseph Ellicott, father of
gifted Andrew Ellicott (one of the founders of Ellicott's Mills, now
Ellicott City). This remarkable clock had four faces. It played many mel-
odies of that era. In Andrew Ellicott's house, a special hall was built
to house and show off this clock.

Time Is Relative

"Theory of relativity" is a phrase usually associated with one or the
other of Albert Einstein's two history-breaking and history-making descriptions of the universe. Yet the word "relativity" applies quite well
to our ordinary everyday ideas of time. Several comments which follow
may make this clear.

"A Funny Thing Happened In North Conway"

This headline, in the July 18, 1965 issue of This Week Magazine
described what happened when everyone in a little New Hampshire town

(Continued on Page 57)

Artists And Craftsmen (Cont'd)

On a sunny day, "solar time" was convincingly demonstrated by this sundial, formerly on the Fayette Street wall of an old Baltimore building located at a busy downtown intersection: Howard and Fayette Streets. "Solar time," although it differs slightly from our familiar "clock time," never "runs down" and is accurate enough for most ordinary purposes. The business firm occupying the building, as a postscript, stated that its methods were "correct" and "on time" every day in the year.

This sundial (on the side of an old tannery building at the Shriver homestead, Union Mills, Maryland) has "marked time" for almost a century. Our colonial ancestors used a somewhat similar idea by marking the daylight hours on a window-ledge strip-just inside a "sunny" window. A vertical window strip (or mullion) thus could "tell time" with reasonable accuracy as its shadow, cast by the sun, moved along the marked-off window. Its central point, sometimes, was the "noon mark."

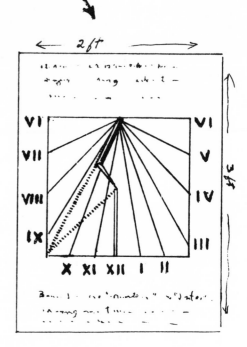

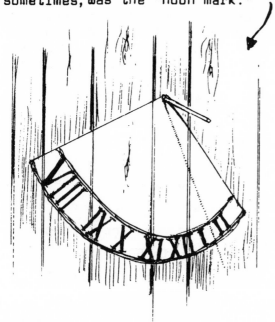

A pocket-size portable sundial (shown in this sketch) was carried by some frontier scouts--- especially those who "counted the hours" until they returned home, safe and sound, to see their sweet-hearts or families, once again. The shadow pointer (called a "gnomen" or "stylus") could be detached, or folded in. Boy Scouts, Girl Scouts, and Campfire Girls of today use somewhat similar pocket sundials.

Artists And Craftsmen (Cont'd from Page 55)

stopped or covered their clocks and watches. This was done from midnight, May 25, until 9 P.M., May 27. Without benefit of alarm clocks, the 1,104 inhabitants went about their daily duties. They had no means of "watching the clock," (and had agreed not to check their TV and radio sets). Surprisingly, 238 of 240 grammar school students reached school almost an hour earlier than usual. The school principal, Mr. William Mathurin, said:

"When the only clocks around are in their stomachs, the kids get hungry earlier. It must have been around 11 o'clock when we served lunch yesterday."

Meanwhile most employees were reporting unusually early for work. A local insurance man, worrying about an 11 A.M. appointment with Sherman Adams, arrived at his Lincoln, New Hampshire home well before breakfast-- at 8:30 A.M.

Crabs Know the Timing of Tides

Unlike overly eager human beings, however, the fiddler crab has a truly marvelous built-in time-keeping arrangement of his own. He shows the time of day by the color of his skin - dark by day, pale at night. Biologists, recording the time of day when the color is darkest, discovered that this occurs 50 minutes later each day than the day before. This seems to be in tune with the rhythm of the tides. For any one crab, they also found, the greatest darkening of color occurred precisely at the time of low tide on the beach where the crab was caught.

The equally-famed Maryland crab has a similar, (and equally-dependable) "built-in" timing system. Through the kind interest of Dr. L. Eugene Cronin, noted Maryland biologist, the following information has been supplied to the authors by one of his associates, Mr. Robert L. Lippson, Crustacean Biologist. He writes:

"Low tide at Solomons, Maryland (site of the Chesapeake Biological Laboratory) occurs four hours later than at Point Lookout (mouth of the Potomac River). This offers no problems for Maryland crabs. No matter what their location may be at the moment, crabs from Solomons Island will unfailingly be darkest about four hours later than crabs from the Point Lookout locality."

In somewhat this spirit, Annapolis had a regulator clock for many years. Other town clocks were set by it. But, in an opposite spirit (perhaps of the North Conway experiment) exact time measurements meant less to many people in Early Maryland. Living closer to Indians and their ways of thinking, they may have agreed with the Indian Chief who said:

"White man has a clock to tell him when he is hungry."

# # #

Getting Up--- "Betimes"

How did people arouse themselves from sleep, in the days before alarm clocks were in general use?

This question has puzzled the authors of this book, for years. "Getting up early" ("betimes," Samuel Pepys phrased it) was necessary for many of those who worked long hours. As for wilderness wanderers, it is hard to picture either George Washington or Thomas Cresap carrying a folding travel alarm clock when heading toward Wills Creek and "The Forks Of The Ohio."

Various authorities, when asked, have given rather unsatis-factory answers, such as: "They went to bed early," or "ser-vants awakened them." Perhaps so, but then, how were the ser-vants awakened? And, on dark dull mornings, what were the arrangements made by those who had no servants?

Two correspondents, partially quoted below, have given very informative answers based upon scholarly research of a high order:

A) "There were alarm clocks in the 18th century during the colonial period... The inventory of the estate of Edward Pugh of Norfolk County, Va., recorded in October 1773, includes the item of one alarm clock valued at 50 shill-ings. However, alarm clocks were evidently rather costly, and probably rare. I imagine that people who had no ser-vants, and were not served by a night watchman (or in other words, most people) simply formed a habit of awaking at a suitable hour, as many people do even now."

      (included in a letter from Mr. Edward M. Riley, Dir-ector of Research at Colonial Williamsburg, Virginia)

B) "Some of the earliest clocks known, dating from the 14th century, were alarm clocks, and there is every reason to believe that some of these were in use in early America. Anyone who lives away from a thickly settled town or city can still rely on birds to wake them at an early hour... It appears that alarm clocks were about the first type of clock to be developed. They were very convenient in mon-asteries to give notice of hours at which prayers were to be said. See pages 15,16, and 17 of The Collector's Dictionary of Clocks by H. Alan Lloyd, published by Country Life Ltd., London, 1964..."

      (included in a letter from the Smithsonian Institu-tion, giving comments by Mr. Edwin A. Battison, Associate Curator, Division of Mechanical and Civil Engineering).

Artists And Craftsmen (Cont'd)

Hand-made --- And "Store Boughten"

"It's hand-made," we may say today, with special pride, about some valued piece of furniture or clothing. Such a remark puts it in a special class, separate from common standardized "machine-made" articles.

Before the war (the one with Great Britain, from 1776 to 1784), most people had almost an opposite attitude. "Hand-made" frequently meant the same thing as "home-made." This, in turn, might mean that a workman or housewife had worked against odds, handicapped by lack of precision-made tools, skill, and suitable materials.

Nearly all "factory-made" hardware, fabrics, and clothing came from England. Besides being well-made, such things were expensive because of shipping costs and taxes.

At the opposite extreme, of course, were all those things "made to order" by skilled professional craftsmen. Many of these would be carried in stock by merchants of today as "ready-made" items---- arranged on counters or shelves, waiting for customers who might want them. Then, however, shoppers knew that storekeepers would have mostly bare necessities (gunpowder, salt, flour, bacon, shovels, and so on), and some few luxuries (loaves of white sugar, perfumes, playing cards, etc.). Beyond this, there were three choices:

A) Make it yourself.

B) Arrange to have it "made to order" by a local specialist.
A planter, for instance, would ride to Baltimore,
Annapolis, or Chestertown, and give a cabinetmaker
instructions for making a new desk or sideboard. A month
or two later, when it was finished, he would make
another trip into town and bring it home.

C) Send an order to England, hoping that the articles
ordered would come "with the next shipment." (With luck,
this would be in four or five months, at the earliest).

(Continued on Page 61)

Artists And Craftsmen (Cont'd)

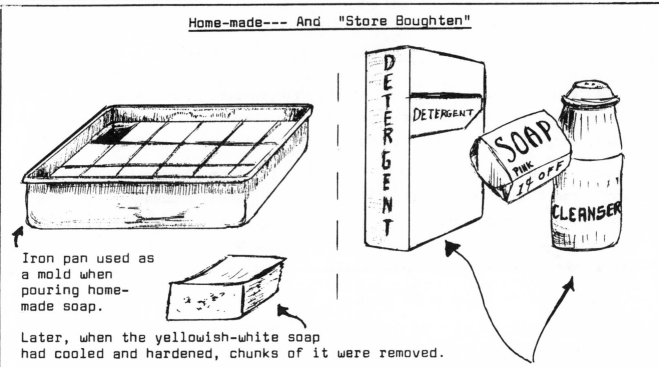

Home-made--- And "Store Boughten"

Iron pan used as
a mold when
pouring home-
made soap.

Later, when the yellowish-white soap
had cooled and hardened, chunks of it were removed.

Those who have made and used home-made soap are best able to appreciate the
convenience and easy cleaning made possible by modern preparations and packaging. Soap chips, in packages, were introduced in 1845 by Benjamin T.
Babbitt. Rather than re-melt waste shavings of soap, he packaged them in 1½
to 2-pound boxes. The idea was welcomed by laundries and hotels. Soap <u>powder</u>
and other "quick" preparations followed.

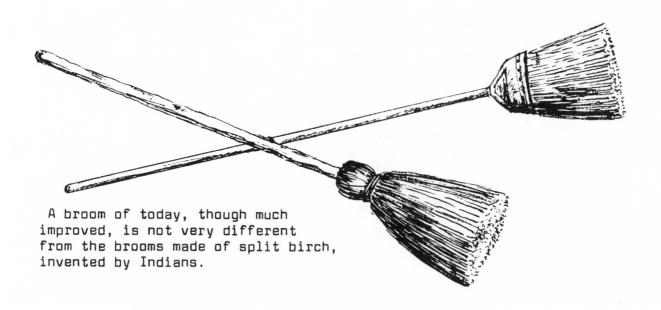

 A broom of today, though much
improved, is not very different
from the brooms made of split birch,
invented by Indians.

Artists And Craftsmen (Cont'd from Page 59)

The wealth of many Marylanders consisted largely of food or tobacco grown nearby; of livestock; and of things made at home. A man (other than well-paid professional people, plantation owners, working craftsmen, and government officials) might need to work hard for several days before he had enough corn, dried fish, tobacco, beaver skins, or lumber to trade for a well-designed factory-made English chisel or hatchet.

The Best--- Is What We See Today

Today, when we see fine pieces of furniture, pewter, or silverware, made by colonial craftsmen, it is well to remember that only the best things (naturally) have been saved, and handed down as heirlooms (or given to museums). The poorly-designed and roughly-made possessions have been junked. Therefore, neither museum exhibits nor antique shops should lead us to believe that beautiful workmanship and fine materials were to be found, customarily, in colonial-era households.

The truth, then, is that those who were wealthy could afford to pay relatively high prices for merchandise of superior quality. Poor people could not.

Some Frontier Settlers Could Afford Luxuries

Jonathan Hager, living at the site of present-day Hagerstown, was a frontier settler, for many years. We might mistakenly conclude, from this, that his house furnishings and clothing would be little better than primitive. But he was prosperous--- not only because of his fur trade, but also because of his thriving real-estate business. (Today, perhaps, we might call him a "promoter"--- and he would very likely be President of his local Chamber of Commerce). There need be no surprise at finding in his restored home (or in the nearby Hager Museum) some gorgeous waistcoats and the very best imported silver and chinaware.

Meanwhile, at that very time--- back in eastern towns and on small farms-- many a family undoubtedly struggled along with cheap "linsey-woolsey" garments and roughly-made furniture or kitchen equipment.

Explanations of 68 old occupations which may not be readily understood nowadays (cartwright, chapman, cobbler, cooper, cordwainer, currier, etc.) are included in a section:

Tradesmen and Craftsmen, of Volume 4, The Greenberry Series
On Maryland (together with suggestions for further reading).

#####

Chapter 8

Food And Drink

"No man need starve who could bait a hook or pull a trigger," Benjamin Franklin once said, speaking of his own time.

In the woods, fields, and marshes, there were wild ducks and geese; snipe; reed-birds; pheasants; quail; and many other kinds of game. In the streams and rivers, there were plenty of oysters, clams, and crabs; bass and rock-fish; shad; drumfish; perch; and diamond-back terrapin.

The woods, too, offered summertime harvests of blackberries and huckle-berries; and then there were persimmons, black walnuts, chestnuts, beech-nuts, and hickory nuts to be gathered in autumn. Cattle, sheep, and hogs had been imported, adding to the supply of meat which could be preserved for winter use, by salting and smoking. Vegetables such as cabbage were brought from the Old World and planted, being welcome additions to the typically American vegetables such as corn, squash, and pumpkins.

Why Others Suffered From Hunger

Actually, the terrible suffering and high death rate in the earlier settlements at Plymouth and Jamestown were partly due to bad planning. For instance, the Plymouth colonists had brought with them fish hooks which were too large for their purpose. The Virginians started their settlement at Jamestown near the end of May--- too late to be really successful in planting and raising crops. It was December before the Puritans landed at Plymouth. The winter months, naturally, are not the best ones for hunting and fishing. Marylanders, from the start, had learned from the mistakes made by others, and arranged to have sufficient food to carry them through each winter.

Herbs And Spices

Spices and dried herbs were in great demand. This was because they gave flavor to the dried, salted, smoked, and pickled foods which were not likely to "spoil" and therefore could be used all through the winter. Meat and other such foods were not always fresh-- far from it.

Food Canning

History, strange as it may seem, states that there was no canned food until Napoleon Bonaparte offered a prize of 12,000 francs in the late 1700's. He had not been talking idly when he said:"An army travels on its

(Continued on Page 64)

Maryland rivers, fields, and woods have always offered many different
kinds of food (as partially indicated in this sketch of purposely
distorted proportions).

Food And Drink (Cont'd from Page 62)

stomach." The prize, therefore, was offered for a method of preserving
fruits and vegetables so that they would have flavor, and yet would not
spoil. A Frenchman named Francois Appert won the prize, after ten years
of experiments. It was not until about 1825, however, that most American
housewives had learned how to do this. (See booklet: "Food And Science--
Today And Tomorrow," by W.G. Darby, M.D., and Gwen Lam. Public Affairs
Pamphlet No. 320, 22 E. 38th Street, N.Y. 16).

A List Of Some Foods That Wouldn't Spoil Quickly

1) Dried: Beans, peas, hominy, rice, oats, etc; Raisins; Apples,
peaches, and other such fruits. Also "jerked beef." Meat
could be preserved, for use on journeys, by drying thin
strips in the sun. This was hard to chew, and had little
flavor. Yet, besides giving nourishment, it permitted
travelling without lighting a campfire-- in Indian territory.

2) Spices: These helped to preserve foods.

3) Sausage: Another way of keeping meat was to grind it for sausage,
adding salt, herbs and spices.

4) Freezing: Our colonial ancestors preserved chickens, turkeys,and
other fowl, during winter months, by allowing them to
freeze, out-of-doors.

5) Packed in salt: Eggs. They could be kept, in this way, through
most of the winter. The packed dry salt prevented air
from passing through the egg shells.

6) Packed in brine: Sauerkraut (shredded cabbage, allowed to ferment
for a while); Olives and pickles; Pork, Beef, and other
meats.

7) Cured by smoking: Ham and bacon

8) Ground into flour or meal: Wheat flour, rye flour, cornmeal, etc.

9) Kept in vinegar: Pickles, etc.

10) Cooked with sugar and spice: Apple Butter

11) Protected by shells or skins: Nuts; lemons, limes, etc.(though
citrus fruits were "luxury" items, even at seaports such
as Baltimore). Coffee beans.

Tea, Chocolate and Coffee

No man need go hungry if he could do as Benjamin Franklin suggested.
Yet it was not always easy to have a variety of foods, especially during
winter, and some of them were expensive. This was true of tea, which
according to various reports, was introduced to the colonies about 1700.

(Continued on Page 66)

Food and Drink

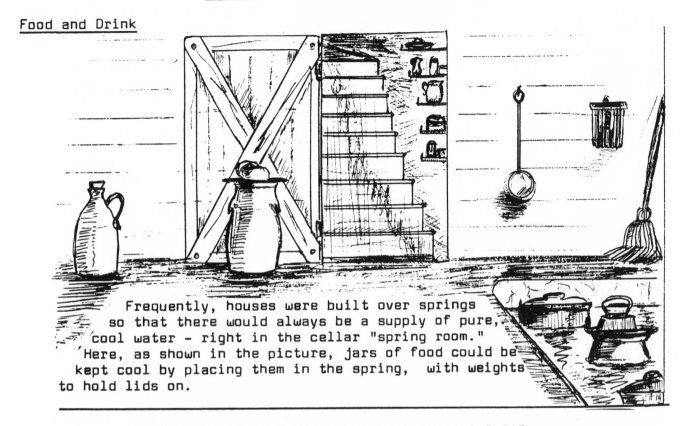

Frequently, houses were built over springs
so that there would always be a supply of pure,
cool water - right in the cellar "spring room."
Here, as shown in the picture, jars of food could be
kept cool by placing them in the spring, with weights
to hold lids on.

EQUIPMENT USED FOR MAKING MAPLE SYRUP AND SUGAR

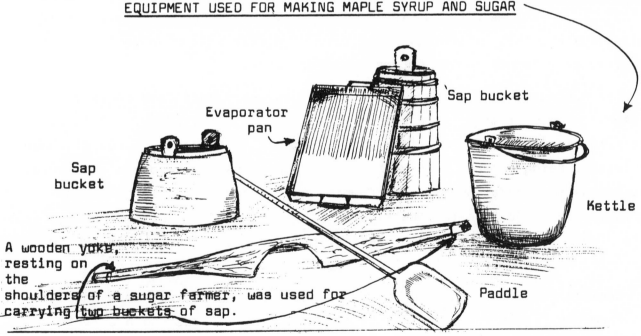

Sap bucket

Evaporator pan

Sap bucket

Sap bucket

Kettle

A wooden yoke,
resting on
the
shoulders of a sugar farmer, was used for
carrying two buckets of sap.

Paddle

Since white sugar was both expensive and scarce, maple syrup from Western Maryland and Pennsylvania were useful for sweetening food. In spring, sap was gathered from sugar maple trees by cutting a hole through the bark, and allowing the sap to drip into buckets. Then, after long cooking in a large kettle, it became syrup - or still longer, it became sugar. Thirty-five gallons of sap are needed to make <u>one</u> gallon of syrup, according to Mr. L.W. Brenneman of Accident, Maryland.

<u>Sugar-making</u> - "To be sold, Lot of ground one acre, with tan yard and several improvements in city of Annapolis, lying on good landing, valuable, well-adapted to business of sugar-making. Apply Thomas Hyde." <u>Maryland Gazette,</u> January 31, 1782.

Food And Drink (Cont'd from Page 64)

Chocolate, strangely enough, was more popular when served as a drink than in any other form. For a time, cups of steaming "hot chocolate" were more popular than either coffee or tea. Sugar, syrup, or molasses, to sweeten these drinks, came from the West Indies islands, although (unknown to many, nowadays) a considerable amount of maple syrup and sugar (then, and now) would come from Western Maryland. (See illustration). The tea, coffee, and chocolate were imported from Europe. In America, these "light drinks" became favorites, especially in the "coffee houses." Of course, there were plenty of people, however, who preferred to drink something stronger, such as rum, brandy, wine, beer, or ale.

Chocolate for cooking, and as a candy, was probably not popular until about 1765. Then the first chocolate to be made in North America, in the form of bars, was produced by John Harmond at Dorchester Lower Mills, on the Neponset River, Massachusetts. Later, this business became Walter Baker and Company, Ltd., now a familiar name to most cooks.

Other Drinks

Bad sanitary conditions in Great Britain and Europe had made water unsafe to drink, in many localities. However, most Americans drank water, at first, simply because they had nothing else to drink. Then they found (miracle of miracles!) that water agreed with them! Before long, however, alcoholic beverages such as cider, wine, beer, brandy and rum became more plentiful and less expensive. These were used more extensively, then, and a great many people really became "hard drinkers."

Some non-alcoholic drinks, and light wines, were made from cherries, peaches, roots of trees, blackberries, persimmons, birch bark, and elderberries. Foods as well as drinks were sometimes sweetened by honey although molasses, being cheaper, was much used by poorer people. Records of special occasions also refer to the use of white sugar shaped into large cones, probably imported from the West Indies. This was used at parties, and at the dinner tables of prosperous people, but sugar cutters (now collected as antiques) were needed to cut off small pieces.

Recipes for drinks, and specimens of new fruit varieties, were passed on from one friend to another. This pleasant custom, added to a certain friendly rivalry, helped immensely to improve the flavor and quality of fruits as well as the drinks made from them.

Breakfast was served late on most plantations--- usually not until about nine-thirty--- and so the planter prepared himself for his morning work by drinking a glass of rum and water, or something similar. An ailment known as gout was common among the well-to-do of the times,

(Continued on Page 68)

...FOOD AND DRINK (cont'd)

Detail of "pot hooks" and "trammel" - used for raising and lowering pots on the crane.

A Cake Mold or "Turk's Head" with handle - Molds were made in many different shapes- of tin, copper & crockery.

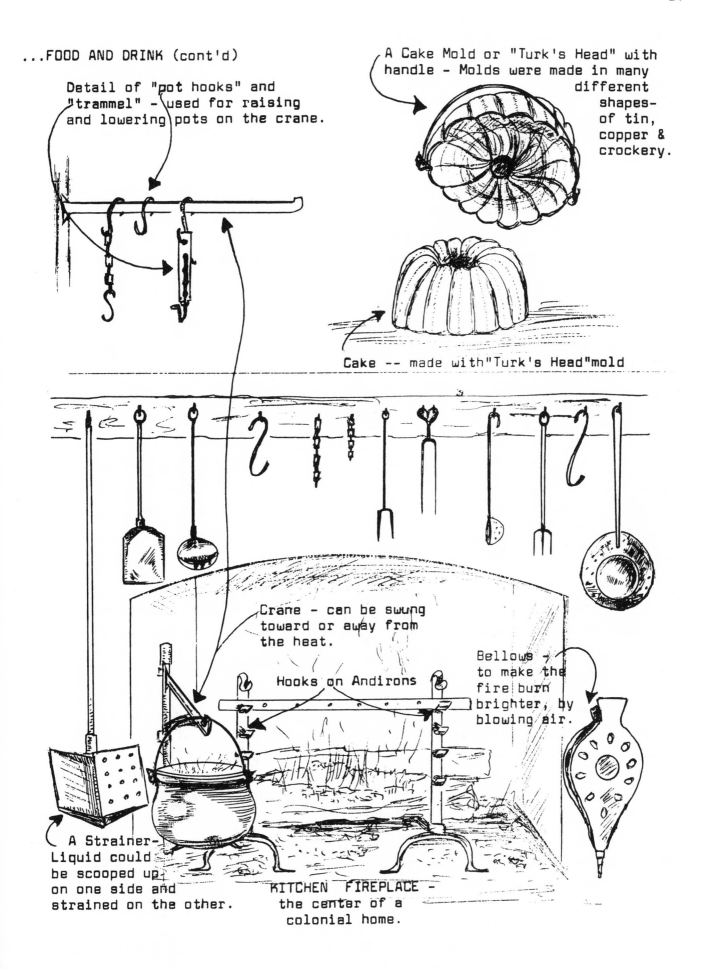

Cake -- made with "Turk's Head" mold

Crane - can be swung toward or away from the heat.

Hooks on Andirons

Bellows - to make the fire burn brighter, by blowing air.

A Strainer- Liquid could be scooped up on one side and strained on the other.

KITCHEN FIREPLACE - the center of a colonial home.

Food And Drink (Cont'd from Page 66)

caused by over-drinking and over-eating.

Tomatoes

With food and drink as with other matters of colonial times, one's wealth and one's station in life made a difference. Bountiful meals and well-stocked food storage bins were the rule on the plantations and in other prosperous households. Elsewhere, food was likely to be simple,plain, and somewhat monotonous, except during the growing seasons. Tomatoes, strangely enough, were generally considered poisonous and were not eaten until about 1830. Before then they were called "love apples," and were grown as ornamental plants.

Pineapples

The pineapple, on the other hand, became a symbol of hospitality after being introduced in England during 1657. Cromwell received one as a gift, and important guests were often given one to take home. Because of this association with hospitality and entertaining, artists, architects, cabinet-makers and silversmiths used it quite often in their designs.

Ways Of Cooking

Since cooking was performed at an open fire, roasting and stewing were the two commonest methods. Roasting was done on a "spit" (sharply-pointed iron rod). Stews were prepared in either brass or iron kettles. These hung from a crane which could be swung backward or forward, to bring the pots either nearer or farther from the fire's greatest heat. (See illustration). Other pots, and most frying pans ("spiders), had iron legs so that they would not sink too deep into the ashes. In large houses, bake ovens some-times were built, on one side or the other of the fireplace and chimney.

Management and control of the fire was one of the secrets of success in fireplace cooking. For instance, no cook would have thought of trying to melt butter over a roaring fire. Instead, she would have raked a little of the fire forward on the hearth. To "regulate the heat" she would have raised or lowered the cooking pots, or covered part of the fire with coals.

"I never understood why so much boiled pudding used to be served" it has been said by Mrs. Helen Duprey Bullock, an expert on early American cooking, "until I used early American cooking utensils. It took so much time to look after the meats and vegetables and soups that a dessert that would just boil along by itself was heaven-sent!"

Food And Drink (Cont'd)

An idea of additional cookery problems is given by Mrs. Bullock's statement that Martha Washington supervised the sweeping of the chimneys, every
Friday, so that no soot or grease which collected there would fall into one
of the cooking pots below.

Ashes Used For Making Soap

Whenever the fireplace was cleaned out, all the ashes were emptied into
a "leach barrel." To produce lye, water was "leached" through this barrel
of ashes; the liquid lye thus produced was saved until soapmaking day. Then
it was boiled in a kettle,(See Page 47) and mixed with quantities of strained
kitchen fats which had been saved for this very purpose, to make soap.

Dishes, Table Silver, And Kitchen Utensils

When served, food was likely to make its appearance on wooden "trenchers"
(wooden plates) or on pewter plates. China dishes and table silver were
found, for the most part, only on the tables of the rich. Forks were not
used by everyone until well into the 18th century. Since the inns usually
furnished spoons but no knives or forks, many travelers carried their own
knives and forks, in leather cases. Not only spoons but drinking vessels,
as well, were made from pewter, although wooden tankards (large mugs or
cups) also served for drinking. Gourds were grown and used, not only for
this but as dippers. Until direct trade with China was started, following
the Revolution, there were china plates, cups, and saucers on few tables.
Many kitchen utensils, such as potato mashers, were made entirely of wood.
Churns, apple-peelers, cherry-pitters, and cabbage-choppers, though operated by "muscle power," produced surprisingly good results.

Famous Food Traditions Of The Region

Maryland, known from its earliest days as a "land of pleasant living"
has always been identified with certain typical delicacies. The Chesapeake Bay region has given us soft-shell crabs, crab cakes, and steamed
hard crabs; oysters and soft-shell clams; diamond-back terrapin; canvasback duck; planked shad, and shad roe. Western Maryland, long ago, originated "apple leather" (a sort of compressed, well-preserved, leathery
apple candy), and persimmon beer. The State, as a whole, has won lasting
fame for Maryland beaten biscuit and Maryland fried chicken. These, and
other dishes from Virginia, Delaware and Pennsylvania, have added
many treasured recipes to cookbooks of the world.

########

Chapter 9

Heating And Lighting

Problems of heating and lighting were quite frequently solved, during colonial days, simply by going to bed early! Since working days began very early, this was probably a good arrangement for some of the rich as well as for most of the poor. It was Thomas Jefferson who wrote, in a letter to a friend: "The sun has never found me in bed."

Candles were expensive, and the big open fireplaces devoured great quantities of the wood which required so much work to cut. A standard complaint about heating was that people's faces burned while their backs froze. It was for this reason that chimney seats, built along the sides of fireplaces, were considered choice places. Some of the fire watchers have reported noticing that sap at the end of long logs was freezing at the same time that the center of the logs was burning briskly.

Great Quantities Of Wood Were Burned

The amount of wood required for the fireplaces of a large colonial plantation is indicated by this extract from a diary of Philip Vickers Fithian, a tutor at Councillor Carter's plantation, Nomini Hall:

"Mr. Carter has a cart & three pairs of oxen which every Day bring in four loads of Wood, Sunday excepted, & yet these very severe Days we have none to spare; And indeed I do not wonder, for in the Great House, School House, Kitchen, etc., there are twenty-eight steady Fires! & most of these are very large!"
(NOTE: See illustrations and captions describing early development of stoves).

Matches had not been invented in the 1700's. The old bad-smelling and somewhat dangerous sulphur matches dated from about 1827 (and the much-improved "safety" matches were not made in America until about 1911). Kerosene was not introduced until the 1850's. Consequently, every household tried to keep at least one fire going constantly--- so that it would not be necessary to go through the long and tedious task of starting a fire by striking a spark onto tinder (pieces of shredded dry cotton or linen which would burn readily) from flint and steel.

In the 1700's, hand-warmers and foot-warmers were taken along to church and other places. Long-handled covered metal pans, also were used to "take the chill off" cold bed-sheets. All these warmers were simply covered metal pans, made to hold a quantity of hot coals and thus throw out heat. Francis Scott Key's young bride from Annapolis was surprised to find, when she began attending church in Frederick, that: "there was no fire. People carried

Heating And Lighting (Cont'd)

their foot-warmers - wooden boxes lined with tin, some with an iron drawer
which held about a tin cup of hot coals... to keep the feet warm."
    (From "Francis Scott Key, Life and Times," by Edward S. Delaplaine).

Foot-warmer
Holes were cut through it, forming a design and,
of course, permitting the heat to escape.

Living In One Room During Cold Weather

Even as late as the early 1900's, many families spent most of their
spare winter-time hours in one room- the kitchen. There was just one simple
reason for this: the kitchen was the only room in the house which was really
warm! Here, therefore, the whole family gathered to read, knit, embroider
samplers, study lessons, crack open nuts they had gathered, pop corn, or
play games.

One Way Of Being Warm

Warm clothing offered one of the best ways of getting warm, and staying
warm. This explains the thick woolen materials which were widely used. It
also explains the fact that ladies frequently wore three or four petticoats,
and that their dresses were made from as much as ten or fifteen yards of
material. Clothing, no doubt about it, was worn in generous quantities!

Candles, Lamps, And Pine Knots

Frontiersmen, and the less prosperous people, managed to produce a
flickering light by burning some large pine knots on flat stones in a corner of the fireplace. Many fireplaces, indeed, were white-washed inside so
that more light would be reflected into the room.

In the northern colonies, glass lamps which burned whale-oil came into
use before the Revolution. In 1787, Richard Henry Lee wrote to his cousin

(Continued on Page 73)

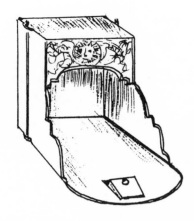

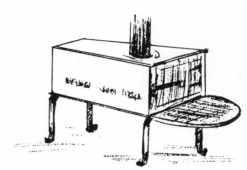

A Franklin wood-burning fireplace (as Franklin called it), made in 1750. By designing this type of heating device (about 1742) he made it possible to save fuel yet get much more heat. This was accomplished by an inside "baffle" which compelled hot gases to circulate somewhat before being lost. Heat radiated into a room from three sides of this "Franklin stove" (as it is usually called). Wood fires in fireplaces, on the contrary, sent most of their heat "up the chimney."

One of the later improvements. In this "six-plate" (box) stove, the main part consisted of six cast-iron plates, bolted together. Manufactured about 1760, in Pennsylvania, this one permitted cooking on the stove's top, besides heating a room. Later, improved wood-burning or coal-burning stoves had ovens for baking, water tanks for heating water, grates through which ashes could be sifted and then removed, as well as devices for using more heat from the smoke before it was lost "up the chimney."

LIGHTING EQUIPMENT RANGED FROM THESE SIMPLE EVERYDAY TYPES TO ELABORATE CHANDELIERS HOLDING MANY DOZENS OF CANDLES.

The hook was used for hanging it.

BETTY LAMP - gave light produced by a wick, usually soaked in whale oil or grease.

CANDLESTICK - with its own CANDLE SNUFFER

CANDLEWICK TRIMMER

One or two candles were fastened inside.

Pierced tin LANTERN (or LANTHORN)- which could be carried from place to place, out-of-doors.

Heating And Lighting (Cont'd from Page 71)

in England: "You will very much oblige me by getting for me one of the most improved Modern Lamps of polished Tin, such as Doctor Franklin brought over with him for giving great splendour of light to a Parlour where company sit. If, in order to use this Lamp, any explanation is necessary, let such explanation accompany it."

Whale-oil lamps of this sort gave more light than candles, but the candles (usually made of tallow) were more generally used in such Middle Atlantic colonies as Maryland.

Do-it-yourself Tallow Making-- Western Maryland Style

One way of making tallow has been described by a hunter of the early 1800's. His description is in a 400-page book (c. 1859, Lippincott) entitled: "Forty-four Years Of The Life Of A Hunter, being reminiscences

(Continued next page)

Fortunate was the early craftsman who had one or more "shoemaker's windows" (also called "lacemaker's windows").

These globe-shaped glass optical devices, when filled with water, could be placed near a sunlit window or several lighted candles. From these they would gather light and concentrate it on a working area.

(Some of these can be seen in the bootmaker's shop at Old Salem, Winston-Salem, North Carolina).

Heating And Lighting (Cont'd)

of Meschach Browning, A Maryland Hunter, Roughly Written Down By Himself."
On Pages 78-9, Mr. Browning tells about killing "the largest panther I ever
saw...

> I took from this fellow sixteen and a half pounds of rendered tallow.
> It is something softer than mutton tallow, but by mixing it with one-
> fourth of its weight of beeswax, it makes good candles."

The cost of using a single tallow candle for five hours of every evening was about eight dollars a month, according to calculations made by the
President of Harvard College, in 1761, and the cost of a spermaceti candle
was about twice as much. Other types of candles, made from the wax of
myrtle and from beeswax, also were used. Spermaceti, (a waxy solid taken
from a whale) was used for making the most expensive candles. These gave
about three times more light than tallow candles, but were more widely
used in New England than in the South.

########

Realizing that daylight would be the best light (as well as the
cheapest) for their purpose, five silversmiths or watchmakers
could make use of a work-bench like this. Thus all five could
perform their delicate work while sitting quite near a window.
Metal-filings and other bits of material, caught by the leather
pockets or by a latticed floor, could be gathered later (perhaps
to be melted, and used again).

(Illustration adapted from Diderot's Encyclopedia, published
1747-1772, in France).

Chapter 10

H O U S E S

Of all the buildings erected in 18th-century America, few remain. One reason for this is that the means of fighting fires were generally poor, resulting in a high rate of destruction. The Great Fire of London in 1666, so well described in Samuel Pepy's famous diary, was a large-scale illustration of what happened in many an American town. The flames spread from one building to another.

Other buildings were torn down just to make room for newer ones or for parking lots. When this happened, it was seldom thought worthwhile to save the smaller houses, typical of the homes occupied by working people. Therefore, most of the 18th-century houses which are now open to visitors actually were once the homes of _wealthy_ citizens. Yet many a working-class family of colonial times considered itself fortunate to live in a house having only three or four rooms.

The "Sorry" House

A pioneer colonist, lacking time and materials to build "in style" would very likely erect a roughly but quickly constructed "sorry house." Jonathan Hager did this, before building his fine substantial stone dwelling now open to visitors, in Hagerstown. (See listing of "Places To Visit," at the end of this book).

"Raising The Roof" - And Adding Wings

Quite frequently, it was necessary for the house to grow as the size of the family grew. Time and again, the owner of a small house would actually "raise the roof," so that two or three upstairs rooms could be added. Looking at old houses, those with sharp eyes often can see faint but telltale evidence of this, especially in brickwork.

Reasoning a bit further, in this way, we might think that wings were also later additions, for much the same reason. In some cases, this is true, explaining the "telescope" style to be seen, now and then, on house and garden tours. Yet there is evidence to show that wings, in quite a number of instances, were actually a part of the original construction, rather than afterthoughts.

Shriver House, Union Mills, Maryland

A really surprising example of the extent to which an old building can grow is offered by the Shriver House, at Union Mills. (This family homestead, chockful of interesting items, and a nearby mill, are open to visitors, at nominal admission, Mon-Fri, 10 to 5; Sunday, 1-5). The original

(Continued on Page 77)

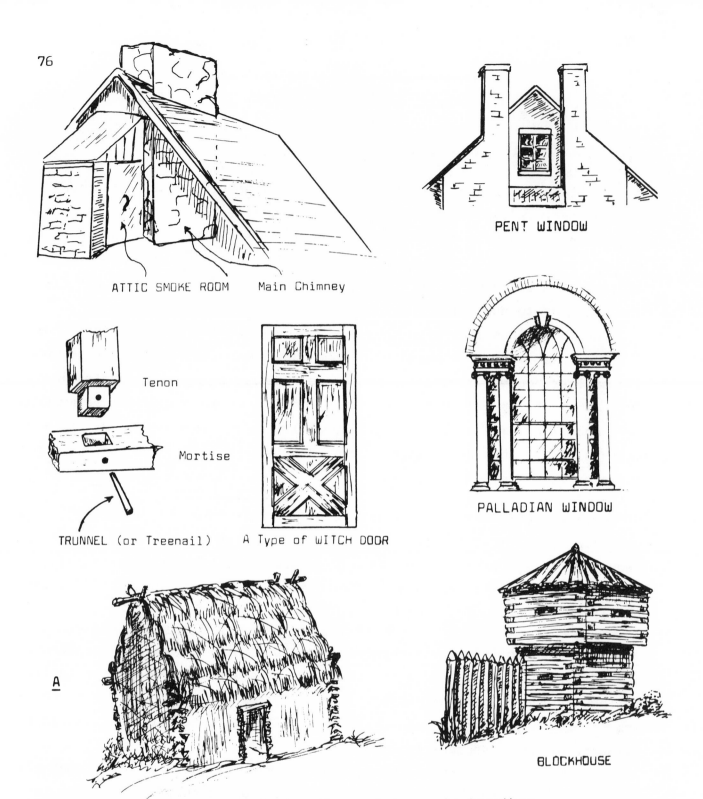

ATTIC SMOKE ROOM   Main Chimney

PENT WINDOW

Tenon

Mortise

TRUNNEL (or Treenail)   A Type of WITCH DOOR

PALLADIAN WINDOW

A

BLOCKHOUSE

A A dependable means of <u>fastening</u> the various parts together is essential in all kinds of building. When the early settlers imitated the Indian method of making wigwams, they used wild tough vines (grape vines or Virginia Creeper) to "thatch" the roof (tie branches, brush, or straw, in overlapping layers, to shed rain or snow). Later, even when stone or wooden construction was used, tying "thatch" onto the roof was often used. Still later, wooden and even slate shingles formed the roof.

B This method of saddle-notching logs at the corners of a building was probably learned from the Swedes. It became common practice on the western frontier where trees were plentiful, but nails, tools, and elaborate building materials were scarce.

B

Houses (Cont'd from Page 75)

portion, having only four rooms, was built in spring of 1797 by Andrew and David Shriver, founders of the community which still bears the name of their mill. During a century or more, one addition after another brought the house to its present size of 23 rooms. The oldest section was built of squared oak logs, chinked with clay. Since the Shrivers "seldom threw anything away," the furnishings "hold a mirror to almost every period of Maryland's growth," including a "parlor barrel organ" almost alongside an old Swiss music box, and an early model spring-driven "Victrola."

Chimneys And High Ceilings

Both heat and cold affected the designs of houses. With the idea of using every bit of heat, chimneys of many Western Maryland houses were placed inside, near the center. In each such case, the house would really be built around the chimney. In numerous other instances, it is true, chimneys in those western areas have been placed at the ends. Yet, so far as old buildings are concerned, it will be noticed that they were nearly always "set in," and not projecting outside the walls. No doubt, here again, a principal reason was that of keeping heat inside.

Yet there may have been another reason, lurking in the minds of those who both feared and loved the rugged majesty of mountains and nearby forests. Perhaps they thought of preventing Indians from climbing up these same chimneys, and setting fire to the roof!

The difference between west and east is made apparent when we look at chimneys of colonial houses built in the southern Chesapeake Bay region. There, the cold of winter was not so much of a problem as the heat of July and August. Then, as now, hot summers were genuinely bothersome. It was for this reason that some chimneys were located outside the walls. (The extra-wide chimneys which are noticeable features of some Maryland mansions, resulted from the desire to have many fireplaces but few chimneys). Likewise, high ceilings were used, wherever possible. (One immediately notices this in many old dwellings not only of Southern Maryland and along the Eastern Shore, but also in Baltimore and its neighboring areas). Since hot air rises, the high ceilings give heated air a place to go--- up.

Ice Houses

"Monticello," the beautiful home built by Thomas Jefferson near Charlottesville, Virginia, contains a splendid example of an "ice house." This was a feature of numerous Maryland farms and plantations. Here, the ice cut during winter months was stored. Some ice houses were really "root cellars." This means that they were used to store carrots, potatoes, and other "root crops" in winter. Toward the end of winter, ice would be placed in them for use in spring and summer.

Houses (Cont'd)

Changes Brought By Changing Times

When prosperous people of the 1600's built permanent homes, what could be more natural than to model them after the styles they had already known and admired in "Merrie England?" There was, of course, a "time delay." The introduction of new styles, whether in houses or clothing, always involves some delay. So, looking back, we may notice that prosperous St. Mary's citizens used designs and ideas which were already "old-fashioned," in the London of that era. Quite naturally, changes were made as time went on, by later generations living in those same dwellings. Therefore, seeing these houses today, we will notice that some offer more than one style (and period) of both architecture and furnishings. Furthermore, structures erected at times when one period-style was being replaced by another are usually regarded as "transitional,"(having some features of each).

"Labels" And "Pigeon Holes"

The beautiful Maryland Institute College of Art building, on Mount Royal Avenue in Baltimore, might be labeled, offhand, as "Italian Renaissance." Roaming through the U.S. Naval Academy grounds, visitors could find it equally easy to describe the general architectural style as "French Renaissance." But "labels" of this sort can be "boomerangs." It would also be natural to say that the architectural spirit of Colonial Williamsburg is "William and Mary," because Virginia moved its capital from Jamestown to Williamsburg (1699) during the reign of England's William III. Yet the official Williamsburg guidebook tells us that the public buildings "resist definite classification in a single style" (mentioning Dutch as well as English influences).

Maryland, partly because of being located between widely differing areas of Pennsylvania and Virginia, has always had considerable variety. Indeed, it is exactly because of their many differences that Maryland's buildings (both private and public) are so interesting and distinctive. Where, throughout the world, will we find any building resembling our graceful Capitol, at Annapolis? Are there duplicates, elsewhere, of the lovely old Otterbein Church (1784), Conway and Sharp Streets, Baltimore (considered one of the finest examples of Georgian style in Maryland? Or of strongly Germanic Zion Lutheran Church (1807), not far from Baltimore's City Hall? Or of those steeply-ascending stone houses in Ellicott City?

Guidelines to Early Colonial Architecture
Given only as a starting point, some guidelines in tabular form are given later in this chapter.

"Joiners" of Colonial Times
The workmen called "joiners" who built many colonial structures were really glorified house carpenters, cabinetmakers; but they knew well the "art and mystery" of "joining" the parts of a house. Floor plans?

(Continued on Page 80)

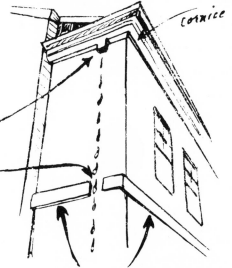

A wooden downspout probably hung from
this opening at the cornice of a noted
18th-century Georgian town house in
Annapolis..... and conducted rain
water to the ground below.

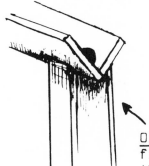

A "belt-course"of bricks---
"set out" from the rest of
the wall--- helped to "break"
the force of overflowing
rain water.

Old-style wooden gutter,
frequently used before
the age of tin or copper.

Water table- usually 2 to 3 feet
above the ground to keep rainwater
from splashing around the foundation of the building.

A brick oven (resembling a
round loaf of bread) sometimes extended completely
outside the chimney,
especially at the end of
a house.

Sliding windows, as seen in Western Maryland houses, (Middletown,principally).
They are arranged to slide along tracks, or grooves, in the wooden framework.
Present-day "home improvement" workmen sometimes install sliding windows when
converting porches into year-round living rooms. They may not realize that
this idea goes back to late 18th-century second-story sliding windows. The
principle is the same, though mass-produced from aluminum.

Houses (Cont'd from Page 78)

Elevations? These were usually taken, ready-made, from books of plans and drawings which could be imported from England. As a matter of professional pride, they generally <u>changed</u> these, to suit their whims of the moment. They also altered them for another and better reason: Because the man paying the bills had ideas of his own concerning arrangements of rooms, windows, and so on.

Northward And Westward--Changes Of Architecture

Moving northward from St. Mary's County we can see, almost mile by mile, early styles of architecture softening and broadening into the more richly-decorated and larger-scale Georgian buildings of Maryland's 18th century. However, while this style was rising to its peak (1740-1775), some completely different ways of building were developing from the Monocacy Valley westward. How could they be so radically different? The reason was simple. Those settling toward the west were mainly of Germanic descent. Some came down from Southern Pennsylvania. Others came by ship from the "Palatine" (mainly German-speaking) regions of Europe. They had no intention of buying slaves and then using their labor to cultivate vast fields of tobacco. Instead, as they or their ancestors had done in Europe, they chose grain and livestock as their main agricultural interests. They and their own families, as a rule, were the ones who did the work. Therefore, their houses, barns, and stables tell us a great deal about this, their chosen way of life.

Georgian Architecture

The "Georgian" style evolved, both in America and England, as a decorative manner of construction based upon the masterpieces of Italian-born Andrea Palladio (1518-1580), and his English-born follower, Inigo Jones.

As progressively developed in Maryland, Virginia and Pennsylvania (with many variations, from the earlier Jacobean, William and Mary, or Queen Anne influences) some features of architectural elegance included (see illustrations):

Palladian (three-part, rounded-arch) windows (named for Palladio). (The gleaming white arches, domes, and columns which Palladio liked to use, were adapted by another of his great admirers, Thomas Jefferson, when he drew plans for the University of Virginia, the State Capital at Richmond, and his own home, <u>Monticello</u>, near Charlottesville).

Bull's eye (round or oval) windows

"Fanlights" and pediments, over doors, or porticoes

Beautifully carved white columns at either side of gleaming white doorways. (These have been adorned, still more, by shining brass--- or even silver--- door knockers, bell pulls, door knobs, or name plates).

Interior cornices (decorative plaster borders, where walls and ceilings of rooms meet. See illustration showing tobacco leaves).

(Continued on Page 82)

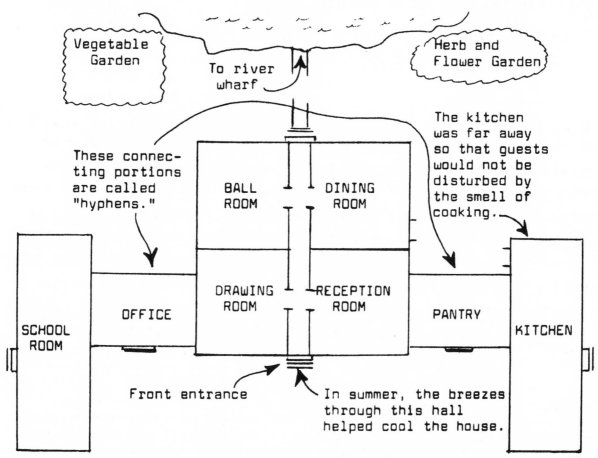

Vegetable Garden

To river wharf

Herb and Flower Garden

These connecting portions are called "hyphens."

The kitchen was far away so that guests would not be disturbed by the smell of cooking.

BALL ROOM

DINING ROOM

DRAWING ROOM

RECEPTION ROOM

SCHOOL ROOM

OFFICE

PANTRY

KITCHEN

Front entrance

In summer, the breezes through this hall helped cool the house.

FIRST FLOOR ROOMS OF TYPICAL LARGE MARYLAND "FIVE-PART" GEORGIAN HOUSE

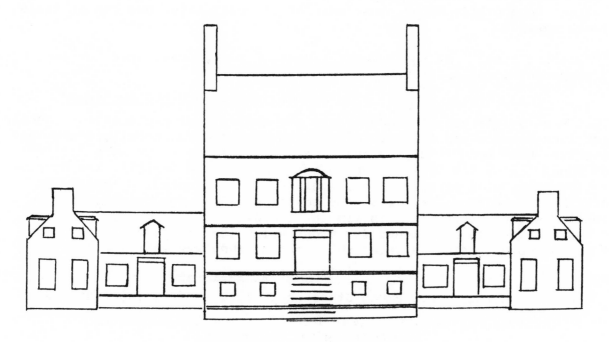

FRONT OF HOUSE SHOWN ABOVE

~~~~~~~~~~~~~~~~~~~~~~~~~~~~~~~~~~~~~~

Houses (Cont'd from Page 80)

Exterior cornices (decorative carved wooden designs, under the over-
hanging portions of roofs).

Carved inside (rather than outside) shutters

"Fancy" patterns of brick

"Five-Part" Georgian House

Many people think that the Georgian style reached its finest
level in the mid-Atlantic "five-part house." (See illustration).
Its general plan could be used for either plantation houses or big town
mansions (built entirely of brick, as a rule). Obviously, it is well suited
for entertaining guests "in the grand manner." It makes possible, for instance, the separation of an elaborate entrance hall, ballroom, livingroom,
and dining room from such necessities of everyday life as the kitchen.

Nevertheless, there is much to be said for the charms and advantages of
other Northern or Southern Maryland, and Eastern Shore dwellings--- re-
lated in spirit if not in actual floor plan. (See table at the end of this
chapter).

"Priest Hides"

"Priest hides" are distinctive features of some 18th-century houses in
Southern Maryland. These "priest hides" are actually secret rooms-- just
large enough to hide one man. For a time, after Cromwell and his Puritans
came into power in England, there was persecution of Roman Catholic clergymen and their followers, even in Maryland, which was originally founded by
Roman Catholics. Then and later, many Catholics, such as Charles Carroll
of Carrollton, had private chapels built into their homes, where they held
services. Doughoregan Manor, just west of Ellicott City, has one of these
private chapels.

Powdering rooms (not the "powder rooms" of today) were used for storing
and powdering wigs, or "perukes."

Secret Tunnels And Hiding Places

Not seen by the casual passerby are the secret hiding-places and tunnels
which lend romance and mystery to some old houses--- especially those near
the water. Once upon time, the shores of the Patapsco River were not far
from Mount Clare, the lovely mansion built by Charles Carroll, the Barris-
ter, (now carefully preserved in Carroll Park, Baltimore). A tunnel, no
longer used, ran from Carroll's home to the water's edge, giving an un-
suspected way of secret exit in time of trouble. In some houses, too, it
was the practice to bury money and other valuables in the cellar or back
yard--- banks not being as dependable then as they are today.

"Hanging Stairways"

"Hanging stairways" are among other especially interesting features of
some fine colonial houses. These have "no visible means of
(Continued on Page 84)

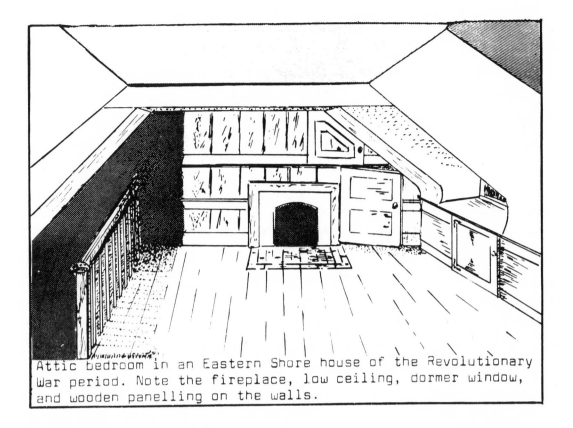

Attic bedroom in an Eastern Shore house of the Revolutionary War period. Note the fireplace, low ceiling, dormer window, and wooden panelling on the walls.

Doorway of a Georgian house in Maryland.

A "hanging" stairway seems to have little support. Hidden iron bars give it strength.

Houses (Cont'd from Page 82)

support" on the sides away from the walls, the necessary strength being given by iron bars projecting from the walls. A beautiful example of a double hanging stairway can be seen in the famous Chase-Lloyd House, Annapolis (open to visitors, year-round, for a small fee). Just above this same stairway is an unusually attractive Palladian window.

Stairs, And "Tree-Nails"

In nearly every case, windows, stair-steps, and other features were not of standard size. Instead, they were likely to vary considerably, according to the carpenter's whim. It was a common thing to go up or down two steps, just to pass from one room to another on the same floor.

Even though it was possible to obtain nails, builders made frequent use of "tree-nails" "trunnels," (or dowels, as we would say today) for fastening boards or other pieces of wood together. (See illustration on Page 76). After holes were drilled to receive them, these rounded pieces of wood were inserted when hot and dry so that they would swell with the addition of normal moisture, thus making the joints hold tight as they aged.

Furniture And House Furnishings

It was Thomas Jefferson who brought to this country the idea of using wallpaper. Previously, walls were either painted, covered with ornamental wooden panels, or left entirely bare. By and large, furniture and draperies of Maryland, in the 1700's, were much like those in England. Queen Anne furniture with its graceful cabriole (or curved) legs, was followed by the somewhat different creations of cabinetmakers such as Chippendale, Hepplewhite, and Sheraton. Probably the greatest cabinetmaker of Maryland was John Shaw, whose workshop was in Annapolis. His sideboards and desks, offering simplicity of design, are now admired so much that their prices run into "five figures."

Carpets, strangely enough, were generally used as coverings for tables

(Continued on Page 86)

A "puncheon" table was made by splitting some logs and using them with the smooth sides up, as shown, supported by four round legs set into holes drilled by an auger. The bench shown was made in the same way. Floors were finished in the same manner as the table top.

CORNICE, USING MARYLAND TOBACCO MOTIF, IN UPTON
SCOTT HOUSE, ANNAPOLIS

CORNICE, ALSO SHOWING TOBACCO LEAVES, IN MARYLAND
STATE HOUSE

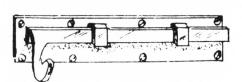

SLIDING LOCK BOLT
(Latch to lock from inside)

WROUGHT IRON
SHUTTER FASTENER

SUFFOLK LATCH
(Arrowhead Design)

KEYS USED THEN
WERE QUITE OVER-SIZED

Houses (Cont'd from Page 84)

and bureaus rather than for floors, until about 1750. Later, not only carpets but painted floor cloths (serving the purpose of present-day linoleum)
became popular. Mats made of rushes also came into use. Kitchens and other
rooms quite frequently had floors made of bricks or pounded clay.

Cupboards And Bathtubs

It was not the custom to plan "built-in" clothes cupboards for houses.
A clothes wardrobe was a piece of furniture placed in some corner of the

(Continued on Page 87)

"Hope chests" may be more an advertising phrase than a reality, today.
But the growing young colonial girl was likely to be serious about such
a thing. In it she collected blankets, tablecloths, sheets and other
"linens" in preparation for her possible married life. Meanwhile the
chest was a strong wooden container which (before feet were added) could
be used as a trunk... if she were obliged to travel. Oftentimes, the outside of her "hope chest" gave a date; initials; and painted or carved designs. Later, as a married housewife, she undoubtedly was annoyed by the
necessity of getting out a blanket from the bottom of her chest. Before
long, someone realized how convenient it would be to add a drawer (with
lock and key) at the bottom---
and then additional drawers.
This led, we are told, to
such now-familiar items
as chests of drawers,
bureaus and sideboards.

Chest of Drawers

Hope Chest

Houses (Cont'd)

room. Somewhere around 1780, housewives began draping curtains to conceal clothing hanging from wooden pegs set into the wall. From this, it was only a step to substitute wooden doors for the curtains.

Water was carried in from the well, in jars or buckets, for every kind of washing, cleaning, and cooking. "Workmen are now busily engaged in removing from the sidewalks in various parts of the city the old worn out and now useless pumps, which have been superseded by the introduction of water from the reservoir..." So said The Baltimore Sun in its May 12, 1862 edition.

Portable metal and wooden foot-tubs and bathtubs were used in colonial times, but it seems unlikely that any built-in bathtubs were in use until the mid-1800's. An octagonal bathhouse of "Trentham," a 200-year old estate in the Green Spring Valley, still contains two bathtubs made of Nicaraguan mahogany. Seven feet long and three feet wide, each tub is lined with metal. Slaves probably brought water from a nearby stream, to fill them, and used heated stones to raise the water temperature.

Mattresses And Beds

Featherbed mattresses, of course, were very comfortable, but a great many mattresses consisted of a "ticking" filled with corn-husks or straw. There was no bed spring. Its place was taken by rope, laced backward and forward around the bed frame. There was an arrangement so that this webbing of rope could be tightened with a wrench, from time to time, when the bed began to sag in the middle. The hangings over a "four poster bed," incidentally, were not for beauty of appearance, but simply to keep out drafts. Going to bed was a mighty cold business, at times, before the days of central heating. Therefore, metal pans filled with hot coals came in handy, on cold nights, to warm the bed sheets in advance.

Cellars - For Food Storage

Cellars, before central heating, were often places for storing food. The name "cellar," itself, comes from the old French word for "food storage room," (celier). Far enough below ground to avoid freezing in winter, cellars were also cool in summer. In many instances, they were not underneath a house, but were entirely separate storage places. A spring room, perhaps only a step or two down from the kitchen, (see illustration on Page 65), would be cooled by water brought from a nearby spring in a hollowed-out wooden trough or pipe. Some dwellings, such as Jonathan Hager's stone house still standing in Hagerstown, actually were built over springs, to provide a cool place for keeping food.

Houses (Cont'd)

<u>Some Among Many Different</u>
<u>Architectural Styles Of Colonial Maryland</u>

From an "embarrassment of riches," several of Maryland's colonial houses
are briefly described, below, emphasizing some features which are interesting either because they are typical or out-of-the-ordinary. Since many
readers cannot make journeys to see them all, page and date references given
refer to issues of the <u>Maryland House and Garden Pilgrimage Tour Books</u>. These
have been chosen because: 1) Most Maryland libraries have them; 2) Illustrations are given in most instances; 3) The information given (much of it de-
voted to Maryland history and numerous other old Maryland buildings) is
dependable. (Except Hampton and Homewood, all are <u>privately occupied</u>).

A) <u>Habre de Venture</u>: This quite unusual Charles County dwelling is
listed first because its three main sections show three distinctly
<u>different</u> kinds of 18th-century Maryland architecture. It was built
and occupied by Thomas Stone, Signer, in 1771. "A Georgian brick
house (is) in the center, flanked on one end by a clapboard struc-
ture once Mr. Stone's law office, and on the other by a frame
building with brick gable ends. To obtain full benefit of the pre-
vailing breezes in the summer and the warmth of the sun in winter,
the three parts of the house were built on the arc of a circle,
connected by differing hyphens. Noteworthy is the 'Great Room' of
classic proportions, the original paneling of which is in the
Baltimore Museum of Art as an example of the finest in Colonial
craftsmanship..." (Picture, p 28; description, p 31, 1952. Description, but no picture, p 24, 1965).

B) <u>Montpelier</u>: (main portion built c. 1720). This fine example of the
Georgian five-part brick house is in that Maryland region having
so many "Homes of the Cavaliers"--- Prince George's County. "The
unusual semi-octagonal design of the wings leads architects to
believe that they were designed by William Buckland, who was re-
sponsible for the strikingly similar Hammond-Harwood House in
Annapolis."

C) An "Orangery" (where colonial gardeners grew oranges and lemons); a
boxwood maze; "Ha-Ha wall"; and bowling green are described under
<u>Wye House</u>, p 58, 1968; the influence of classical Greek design,
in columns and pediments (together with an unusual Georgian
cupola) are shown under <u>Hampton</u>, p 70, 1953, and p 49, 1952. Page
31 of 1952 has a fine picture of <u>La Grange</u>; its main portion
shows a favorite Southern Maryland combination of white clapboard
siding, with brick ends and four <u>outside</u> chimneys. The cover picture of 1952 also shows a five-part Georgian house in Baltimore
City, built by Charles Carroll, Signer, for Charles Carroll, Jr.
It is <u>Homewood</u>, now part of Johns Hopkins University. (Description, p 35)

∧∧∧∧∧∧∧∧∧∧

Not many people had a great house like this one. It is Rose Hill Manor, owned by former Maryland Governor Johnson. It is located at Frederick, Maryland

J. H. Cromwell photograph.

Middleham Chapel; founded in 1684 as a chapel of ease; rebuilt in 1748.

J. H. Cromwell photograph.

~~~~~~~~~~~~~~~~~~~~~~~~~~~~~~~~~~~~~

Houses (Cont'd)

Some Smaller Colonial Buildings Of Maryland

As a matter of convenience to all who may want to see them, the buildings mentioned below are all in one community, Annapolis, capital city of the State. All except one are described in the Historic Annapolis, Inc. Tour Book (c. 1954), and its illustrations give an idea of their appearance. All are now privately occupied.

D) Gambrel-roofed brick story-and-a-half house at 160 Prince George Street. It was the home of Patrick Creagh, builder and contractor, and he probably built it, between 1735 and 1747. Locally, it is known as"Aunt Lucy's Bake Shop"--- for a talented Negro baker, Mrs. Lucy Smith who apparently made and sold, here, some mouth-watering cakes, cookies, and other bakery products. (Map 29, p 16. Also see article: Patrick Creagh of Annapolis, by Joy Gary, pp 310-26, Dec. 1953, Maryland Historical Magazine.

E) The oldest wooden frame building in Annapolis (c. 1690),is the Sands House. A variation of the "salt box" type, it is shown on p 16, Map 29.

F) A restored small wooden frame house occupied by an early Maryland workingman and his family, at 45 Fleet Street.

G) Reynolds' Tavern, of colonial times, on Church Circle. It is built of bricks laid in an interesting "all header" pattern (only the ends showing). Note the decorative water-table (or belt course) above the first-floor windows, which helped to shed rain away from the foundation. Now houses offices of the local Public Library (Map 8 & 9, Page 8).

~~~~~~~~~

The Oldest Stone House In Western Maryland

H) The Hager House ("Hager's Fancy"), built 1739-40, as the home of Jonathan Hager, Founder of Hagerstown, Maryland. (Open to the public, together with the nearby Hager Museum, containing many objects found in or near the house. Nominal admission; student groups and children under 12, free. Open: April to November; Tues-Sat: 10-5; Sun: 1-5; Mon-Closed. Nov-April, by Appt. Guide Service). Captain Hager (who served as a volunteer Captain of Scouts in the 1755 Braddock Campaign) built this dwelling over two springs, still to be seen in the cellar. It served him as a House-Fort and Fur-Trade Post.

At least several hours should be allowed for a visit because of the wealth of historical and background material to be seen here.

~~~~~~~~~~

Interesting Features of Some Western Mid-Atlantic Buildings

A) Gallery (second or third-floor) porches-- reminiscent of those found so frequently in the old town of St. Michaels, on the Eastern Shore.

B) Arched porticoes

C) Circular windows over porticoes or in end gables

D) Extra-wide frames for windows and doors, pinned in place by wooden dowels or "trunnels" (tree-nails,so called).

E) Out-of-doors Dutch Ovens, joined to the house beyond the chimney. (See Page 79)

F) Catslide roofs

G) Two-leaved outside door, also known as a "Dutch door" or "Jib" door. The top portion can be opened, to chat with someone outside, while the bottom portion remains closed, to keep animals from entering the house, and so on.

H) "Pent" windows (See Page 76). Those going on the annual house and garden tours may be a bit inclined to associate these oddities with Southern Maryland and the Eastern Shore. But they will be noticed, here and there, in Western Maryland. The practical side, no doubt, would be that of locating a small room or closet so that, on cold days, the heat of the chimney(or chimneys) around it, would warm it.

I) Double sliding windows. (See Page 79).

J) Mennonite dwellings. These, commonly, have <u>two</u> entrance doors and <u>two</u> staircases, one for men and the other for women.

K) "Bank" barns and "bankside" houses. Just as in Southern Pennsylvania, a great many farmers have built their barns against a mound of earth, or bank. Thus, on the "bank side," horses and wagons or gasoline-propelled vehicles can drive directly onto the second floor of the barn, to load or unload hay, etc. If no convenient mound of earth has existed for this purpose, many a farmer has hauled earth and dumped it to form an arti- ficial hill or bank. No far from Hagerstown is a quite unusual three-story residence built against an earth embankmen

Bank House

Houses (Cont'd)

in such a way that only the third floor can be entered from the road. Leaving the lower floor, one is in a deep valley, quite some distance below the level of the road.

"Bank" barns have another advantage. Since the two-story side customarily faces south, the barnyard, just outside, has some protection against winter storms; also the sun, rising toward the southeast and setting at southwest, melts snow and ice more quickly than elsewhere.

Brick barns. Whether they are built entirely of brick or only with brick ends, the passerby may find it pleasant to notice how many have decorative open brickwork at the gable ends. (Often, "date stones" show initials or names, as well as date of construction).

Stone barns. These are numerous, usually with wooden clapboard sides, and ends built of native field stone.

Distilleries. The old residents had their "brewhouses" for making beer, ale, and light wines, just as William Penn's farm workers did at his Pennsbury Manor (a replica, not far from Philadelphia, is open to visitors). But the name used in Western Maryland was, generally, "distilleries."

Wooden Locks, good evidence shows, were used on main doors of some old houses. The reason? Since other portions of these houses were not "poor," this may have been done by "proud patriots" who hated to pay taxes on imported English hardware.

"Saltbox" houses. There are several attempted explanations of this peculiar construction. Mr. Edwin Tunis thinks (see his Colonial Living, P 33) that the rear portion was really a "linter" (leanto) added to the original small house. Toward the end of the 17th century, new houses were built in that style, intentionally. Others have said that the saltbox sloping roof-line was really an attempt to avoid taxes based upon size and height of a house.

Stone walls. Perhaps because field stone was plentiful, (as in New England) many of these were built, instead of wooden fences. Some of them are still standing. (Fort Frederick is the only original stone fort of the Revolutionary War period which is still in existence. It was once owned by a freed slave, who tore down some of its walls while farming. Portions of the present walls are original; others have been restored. The fort is about 15 miles west of Hagerstown, near the Potomac River, and is open to visitors).

Wattle and clay, (or "wattle and daub") construction. This may remind us of the opening lines in a well-known poem by William Butler Yeats:

"I will arise and go now, and go to Innisfree,

And a small cabin build there, of clay and wattles made..."

The word "wattle" has a British dictionary definition of:
"stakes, sticks, or rods interwoven with twigs and branches of
trees, to make a fence, wall, etc." Pioneer settlers, everywhere,
soon have learned that the quickest way to build is by using this
method, daubing on considerable quantities of wet clay. Hardened
by the sun, this results in a rather satisfactory wall. Using this
"lazy man's method", many settlers of America even built chimneys
in this manner. Later, however, this would be a danger because the
fire's heat would burn out the intertwined wood, leaving little
more than the clay, and many openings from which sparks and embers
might leap out.

Cupola: Although not seen quite as frequently as in the east, a
         cupola is the "crowning glory" of many an old building,
going westward in Maryland. Some are surmounted by a weather-vane,
one being the replica of "Little Heiskell" swinging to and fro on
top the Hagerstown City Hall. Often they have clocks on their sides,
yet they are as graceful as anything in the "Georgian" country of
Anne Arundel or Talbot Counties.

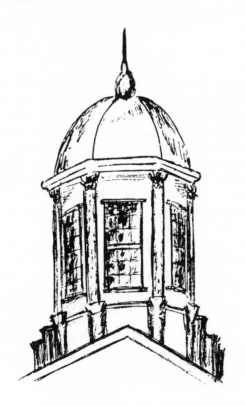

Chapter 11

Clothing

When reading about the fabrics and clothing of the 1700's one comes across many unfamiliar names of materials such as fearnought (or fear-nothing); kersey, or kerseys; Osnabrigs; Padisoy; super-fine drab; and Irish frize (or frieze). Fearnought was a kind of stout woolen cloth, much used because of its durability; kersey (named after Kersey, England) was a compact woolen cloth having a fine nap and smooth surface; Padisoy was a smooth, strong and rich silk fabric; super-fine drab evidently referred to a particular kind of drapery material; and Irish frize was a heavy-napped woolen cloth used for overcoats.

Marks Of Social Standing

Social position, in the 18th century, was usually indicated not only by the "bearing" (general attitude) of a person, but also by the quality and style of clothing. Imported damask, brocade and similar fine quality materials (often with linings) were used in making the best clothing. This was sewn together with expert workmanship, by hand.

"Stays" Worn By Women

For Sunday best, women wore "stays" in their dresses (which did not show). These were whale bones, (later, pieces of steel) sewn inside the garment, at the waistline. They were made to give "support," and good posture. "Staymakers," (who also were tailors) often advertised in the Maryland Gazette:

> "Robert Gordon, Stay-Maker, living near the Town-Gate, in Annapolis... Having just Imported in the Fleet from London, a large Assortment of Stay-Goods (consisting of Tabbies & Whale-Bone of the very best Kind) hereby gives notice to all his old Customers and others... He can now furnish them with STAYS in the newest fashion..."

> Maryland Gazette, Aug. 27, 1761

Clothing For Dress Wear

For dress wear, a man wore a "stock" around his neck, (a sort of white ruffled collar which draped downward, in front). His waistcoat, very large when compared to the vests of today, hung far down on each side. Often, it was embroidered. A "joseph," worn by women when riding, was a long cloak

(Continued on Page 95)

94

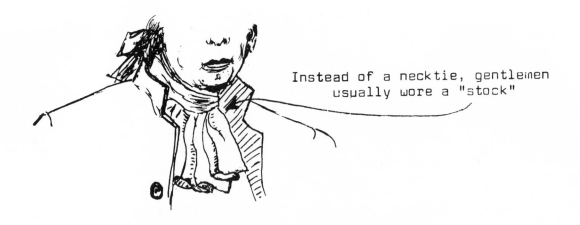

Instead of a necktie, gentlemen usually wore a "stock"

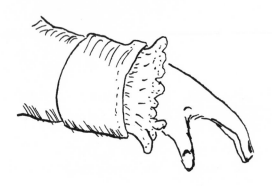

A gentleman's dress shirt had ruffles showing below the coat cuff

Man's buckled shoe

Though dated 1825, this is typical of 18th-century advertisements.

Clothing (Cont'd from Page 93)

with a cape. A "silk hood Capuchin" was a cowl type of hood such as monks wear. "Silk clogs" were shoes intended for dress wear.

Cotton was not yet an important domestic crop. It was expensive because the cotton gin did not come into use until after 1793. Consequently, imported linen was used for underwear, shirts, handkerchiefs, and all such purposes. Manufactured woolen cloth was both expensive and scarce. Therefore, families of farmers wore home-spun garments made from wool. Poor people were accustomed to using articles made of "linsey-woolsey," a mixture of wool and flax. Silk materials were worn almost exclusively by the rich.

(Items in the Maryland Gazette tell of early attempts to produce silk and grow cotton in Maryland, but all these were failures).

Leather Aprons And Trousers

"One misty, moisty morning, when cloudy was the weather,
I chanced to meet an old man, all clothed in leather."

(From an English folk song)

Leather trousers and aprons were commonly worn by laboring men, and these were kept pliable by being oiled and greased. Woolen stockings and heavy cowhide boots or shoes, often supplied with wooden heels, also were worn by workingmen. After 1780, long trousers began to replace knee breeches. In the 1800's, it became an established custom to furnish shoes in "lefts" and "rights." (The first ones were made in Philadelphia, during 1800, by William Young). Previously, most people "switched" shoes each night, in preparation for the next day, so that the shoes would wear evenly.

Measurements

A great deal of "guesswork" entered into measurements when orders for shoes, hats, and working clothes were filled in England. "Whether it be the fault of the tailor, or the measure sent, I can't say," George Washington complained, "but, certain it is, my clothes have never fitted me."

Pioneer Clothing

"On the frontiers, and particularly amongst those who were much in the habit of hunting, and going on scouts... the dress of the men was partly Indian..." So wrote the Reverend Joseph W. Doddridge, when describing the people with whom he lived, during 1773-74. "The hunting shirt was universally worn. This was a kind of loose frock, reaching half way down the foot or more when belted. The cape was large, and sometimes handsomely fringed with a ravelied piece of cloth of a different colour from that of the hunting shirt itself. (See illustration- Chapter 3). The bosom of this dress served as a wallet to hold a chunk of bread, cakes, jirk (jerked, or dried meat), tow for wiping the barrel of the rifle, or any other necessary for the hunter or warrior. The belt which was always tied behind

(Continued on Page 97)

96

A) This shows only one of many dress styles that were popular about 1760.
B) Bonnet worn in the 1700's. C) Parasol- Women used them as sunshades.
C) "Mob cap"- worn in the house. E) Folding fan- used for all occasions.
F) The woman using the butter churn is wearing a common type of 18th century working dress.

Clothing (Cont'd from Page 95)

answered several purposes, besides that of holding the dress together. In cold weather the mittens, and sometimes the bullet-bag, occupied the front of it. To the right side was suspended the tomahawk and to the left the scalping knife in its leathern sheath. The hunting shirt was generally made of linsey, sometimes coarse linen, and a few of dressed deer skins. These last were very cold and uncomfortable in wet weather. The shirt and jacket were of the common fashion. A pair of drawers or breeches and leggins, were the dress of the thighs and legs. A pair of moccasons (sic) answered for the feet much better than shoes. These were made of dressed deer skin.

"The linsey petticoat and bedgown which were the universal dress of our women in early times, would make a strange figure in our days... They went barefooted in warm weather, and in cold, their feet were covered with moccasons, coarse shoes, or shoepacks."

Dyes And Wigs

Since chemical dyes were almost unknown, dyes for coloring linen, cotton, and wool were made from berries, plant leaves or flower petals, and from bark or roots of trees. Many shades of blue came from the indigo plant, a native of the West Indies which was introduced and cultivated in South Carolina. Dark browns and yellows could be produced from black walnut bark; green from hickory; and black from willow. The sumac berry gave shades of gray. Crimson could be produced from poppy petals.

Wigs were standard articles of dress for gentlemen, except on informal occasions, and boys of good families were trained to wear them for all dress affairs. In the "powdering room" the owner of a particular wig (or peruke) would sit with a great cloth wrapped around his neck. He would hold a glass horn, or leather cone over his face-- to keep the powder out of his eyes, as a servant dusted his wig.

Color Became Fashionable

From about 1750 until the American Revolution, there was a pronounced tendency toward warmth of color throughout the colonies- especially in such middle or southern colonies as Maryland and Virginia. This use of gay colors was found not only in clothing but also in decorations of wagons, coaches and miscellaneous belongings. Yellow waistcoats, scarlet coats or stockings, and gowns or veils of emerald green or purple were "quite the thing." These were ornamented by silver buckles, gold or brass buttons, and plenty of jewelry. It was an age of color and decoration, and perhaps this made up, to some extent, for the dim lighting and the poor heating.

#######

Chapter 12
Agriculture

Tobacco was so vital in Maryland and Virginia that the word itself, was frequently abbreviated, thus "Tob^o." "As good as gold" are words that could have described it, because the dried brown leaves of the plant were actually used in place of money, many times, until after the American Revolution. A great many people smoked tobacco daily, usually in pipes, or cigars. Others, however, crushed the dried leaves into a fine powder. They called this "snuff," (carrying it in small snuffboxes) and used it by sniffing a little up each nostril. No doubt, these people enjoyed the smell of the tobacco, and the sneeze which was sure to follow.

Hogsheads (or casks), used for shipping not only tobacco but also liquids, such as molasses or rum.

On its way to distant markets, tobacco was packed in hogsheads (or casks). Each held about a ton. These were made so that axle pins could be inserted. Then, by attaching shafts or drag ropes, the hogsheads could be pulled along by oxen or black slaves.

Advantages Of Growing Tobacco

Tobacco sold for high prices as compared with its light weight and the small amount of space needed for shipment. Therefore, the cost of transportation was very low. This, together with the great demand for it (both overseas and in America) made it a popular crop. There was little fear that it would spoil. Furthermore, large quantities could be grown on just a few acres of land. Finally, having the work done by slaves, it was possible to raise tobacco on many hundreds of acres. It was in this way that large fortunes were made by some Maryland families, such as the famous Lloyd family of Talbot County.

Disadvantages Of Growing Tobacco

For all these reasons, a great many 18th-century farmers wanted to plant as much tobacco as possible. Only from bitter experience did they finally

Agriculture (Cont'd)

admit that this crop was "hard on the soil." Fields which were naturally
"rich" lost much of their growing qualities if tobacco was planted, year
after year. Less and less tobacco could be harvested, they found, and the
quality was not as good. Therefore, following the example and advice of
Charles Carroll of Carrollton, many farmers began to grow less tobacco. He
showed them how to make worn-out "tobacco land" suitable for growing wheat
by applying plaster (lime) and fertilizer. Others who wanted to continue
growing tobacco began to practice what is called "crop rotation." This
means that tobacco would be planted less frequently (perhaps every third
or fourth year), and that other crops, such as clover (adding nitrogen to
the soil), wheat, and corn, would be raised in the other years.

Tobacco Becomes Somewhat Less Important

Gradually, tobacco lost some of its former importance as a road to quick
riches. To this day, however, (aided by use of fertilizer and scientific
cultivation) it continues to be a big "money crop" in the southern counties
of Maryland's Western Shore.

Fruits And Vegetables Which Early Settlers Found Growing In Maryland

Among fruits and vegetables which were already growing on Kent Island
when Captain William Claiborne made his first explorations there, in 1628,
were grapes and corn. Also, there were strawberries and other berries
(such as blackberries); persimmons; peas (or "pulse"); pumpkins; and
squash. Corn ("maize") was an important crop which settlers grew after
learning about it from the Indians. Later, of course, seeds of other kinds
were brought from the Old World and planted. By the late 1700's, therefore,
rather large quantities of wheat, rye, oats, and other plant foods (grown
from imported seeds) were being harvested. On the Eastern Shore, especially,
farmers mostly turned toward raising chickens or other poultry, and
toward melons, tomatoes, various other vegetables, and fruits.

Farming, As Taught By The Indians

Most settlers knew about the Indian method of starting a farm in the
woods. It was the quickest way, and it was easier, at first:

A) They "girdled" each tree and killed it, by cutting away some bark and
outer wood, not far above the ground. Soon, as the tree died, its
leaves withered, allowing the sunlight to pass between the branches.

(Continued on Page 101)

Agriculture (Cont'd)

An 18ᵗʰ-century Plan For Stocking A Farm And Laying In A Year's Supplies

80 acres of land (with cabins)
including 30 acres to be cleared, for
sowing grain
2 plough horses
2 cows, with calves
10 sheep
1 plough, saddles, harness, etc.
A one-horse cart
Household furniture

Also, provisions for one year:
1,000 lb. pork
300 "   beef
40 bushels wheat
3   "   salt
8   "   Indian corn
2,000 lbs. hay
20 bushels potatoes
etc.

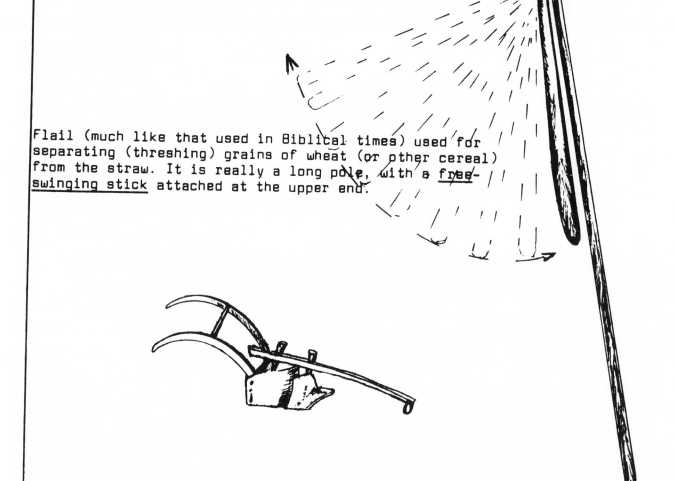

Flail (much like that used in Biblical times) used for separating (threshing) grains of wheat (or other cereal) from the straw. It is really a long pole, with a free-swinging stick attached at the upper end.

A mold-board plow (having a curved shape near its steel point) was a great step forward by early settlers. With it, plowing could be done faster and deeper.

Note: One of many colonial life exhibits in the Smithsonian Institution's Museum of History and Technology states: "In colonial America two men could plow one acre in 12 hours; nowadays one man can plow an acre in 1¼ hours."

<u>Agriculture</u> (Cont'd from Page 99)

B) After that, there was no attempt to plow the soil. Instead, grains of corn (or other seeds) were simply pressed into the ground, here and there--- usually four seeds to a hill. Sometimes, a dead fish was placed into each hill, providing fertilizer as it gradually decayed.

C) Several squash (or pumpkin) seeds, and some beans, were also planted in each hill. Then, as the corn grew, the bean vines would climb up the cornstalks. The squash (or pumpkin) vines would spread out, on the ground, among the hills.

D) After harvesting all crops, in autumn, such a farmer would probably set fire to the dead trees, burning them to the ground.

E) There were, of course, several disadvantages to this Indian method. The tree <u>stumps</u> still remained. Plowing and cultivating could not be done, satisfactorily, until they were removed. Those who liked the thorough methods of German, and other Old World farmers, preferred to cut down all the trees, pull out the stumps, and clear away all bushes, stones, and weeds. Then, using horses or oxen (instead of hand labor with a hoe and rake), they would plow, cultivate, and fertilize. This was, by far, the best way when growing grain, though much time and labor were needed at the very <u>beginning</u>.

Most Farms Were Small

Today we read much about the large plantations of colonial Maryland and Virginia. Actually, most farms were rather small. The work on these was usually done by the owners and their families. Large plantation or small farm, this was hard work and was done slowly, by hand.

The Indian Art Of Making Maple Sugar

Among many valuable lessons learned from the Indians by colonists, was the art of collecting sap from sugar maple trees, and then boiling it until it thickened into syrup (or sugar, after longer cooking). Indian methods were crude, but they warned that the maple sap will not "run":

A) in cold weather (below 30-32°)
B) in warmer weather (around 50°)
C) when the trees are in leaf.

As the first buds began to swell on the trees, the Indians made syrup and sugar "by wounding the trunk of the tree, and placing a receiver under the Wound." A Honey or Sugar-Tree "yields a kind of sap or juice which, by boiling, is made into sugar," so says Robert Beverley's "History and Present State of Virginia," printed in 1705.

The colonists of Western Maryland (and many another more northern locality) were apt pupils. By 1850, <u>cane</u> sugar was being produced in only <u>nine</u> states. Earlier than that, maple sugar was being made in no less than <u>27</u> states, as far west as Minnesota, and in all the Middle Atlantic

Agriculture (Cont'd)

and Southern states except Delaware, Florida, Mississippi and Texas.

In earlier years, when sugar-cane or sugar-beet sweetenings (and even molasses) were not really cheap, maple syrup and sugar were actual necessities. Frontiersmen, especially, had no way of bringing in any helpful quantity of other sugar products - even if they could afford to pay for them. Peter Kalm, early Swedish botanist, wrote (1751): "The common people.. supply themselves with a large quantity of this (maple) sugar each year... Many farmers have whole barrels full... Practically every soldier in the French forts manufactures a year's supply of this necessity for himself, in the spring..." Even today, the annual "sugaring off" (as maple sugar farmers call the operation of sap boiling) is almost entirely a family occupation and a family business.

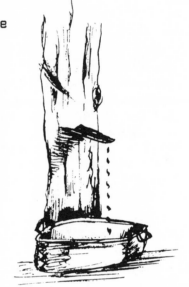

Indian Way Of Gathering Sap

More Work than poetry

Anyone who thinks sugar farming has been, (or is) easy, should read an 1874 report by Mr. E.A. Fish, Vermont Board of Agriculture, who wrote:

"Let one who has used the modern improvements of the mode of our fathers; let him have the caldron kettle, the potash kettle, the five pail and three pail kettle hung on poles, and watch them by day and night, with nothing to shelter him from storms; let the wind blow and fill the boiling sap with ashes and dust, and his eyes with smoke, let him mount his snowshoes and bring in all his sap to the 'boiling place' upon his back,

Sap boiling method in the early days. The storage trough (which held about 4 or 5 barrels of sap) was cut from a solid log.

and if he finds poetry in it, I think he will say, I prefer prose hereafter."

Agriculture (Cont'd)

Yet someone with an inquiring mind could write, as Henry David Thoreau did, in 1893:

"Had a dispute with father about the use of making sugar (sic)... He said it took me from my studies. I said I made it my study and felt as if I had been to a university... (Note: He who carries through all the operations involved in producing maple sugar is a woodcutter, forester, botanist, ecologist, meteorologist, agronomist, chemist, cook, economist, and merchant)."

Much of the data given above has been supplied by the kind help of:

> Mr. L.W. Brenneman (Sugar farmer)- taps 1,000 trees
> Accident, Maryland
>
> Mr. George Keim (Sugar farmer)- taps 5,000 trees
> Keim's Kamp, West Salisbury, Pennsylvania

A fine reference book on this subject is "The Maple Sugar Book" by H. & S. Nearing, (pub. the John Day Company).

Almost Everyone Did Some Kind Of Farm Work

Nowadays, farming is only one way, among many, of earning a living. In colonial times, however, it was a "way of life" for most people, no matter what their main work might be. For instance, schoolmasters and clergymen often were permitted to use pieces of land on which to raise crops for food. This was considered a part of the payment for their services. The usual attitude is show in a sentence written in the diary of a great statesman, John Adams: "Rose at sunrise, unpitched a load of hay, and translated two more leaves of Justinian."

More People - Fewer Farmers

These is reason to believe that considerably more than 60% of colonial America's people were engaged in agriculture. In the late 1600's, the percentage probably equalled that reported by some present-day "emerging" or "developing" regions. For example, the 1968 World Almanac tells us that agriculture occupies 70% of India's people. By contrast, in this same year of 1968, the United States of America--- by use of scientific methods and power equipment--- was able to send many shiploads of food to fill empty stomachs located far beyond the horizon.

Yet, largely because of those same scientific methods, our country, in 1968, considered it necessary to encourage still further reduction of planted acreage. Reliable estimates indicate that only about 5% of American population could be called farmers. (Thus, one farmer, here, would be growing enough food for about 20 other Americans, while also helping to feed a great many of those in misery overseas).

#####

^^

Chapter 13

Money, Manufacturing,and Trade

There are a number of mistaken ideas about some kinds of work done during colonial days. Nearly everyone thinks of a blacksmith as "a man who shoes horses." In the 18th century, however, this was the one thing a blacksmith did <u>not</u> usually do. Horseshoes were made and fitted by farriers. Blacksmiths made other kinds of iron work, such as hinges, latches, and kitchen utensils. It was in the 1800's (when things made of iron were manufactured more cheaply in factories) that blacksmiths gradually began taking over the work formerly done by the farriers. Whitesmiths worked with <u>light-colored</u> metals such as tin, and coppersmiths worked with copper and brass. The word "smith" comes from the word "smite"--- meaning "to strike." Therefore, we can also speak of a silversmith--- one who makes some articles of silver by pounding (or <u>striking</u>) them with a hammer or mallet.

What Some Other Workmen Did

Currier--	one who dresses and colors leather, after it has been tanned
Potter--	one who makes earthen pots and chinaware
Cooper--	one who makes or repairs barrels, tubs, and casks
Joiner--	a carpenter, especially one who constructs buildings, or who makes doors,& windows for them
Sawyer--	one who saws wood, or other materials
Glazier--	one who fits windows with glass panes, etc.
Cutler--	one who makes, repairs, or sells knives, scissors, and other "cutlery."
Millwright-	one who designs, builds, or repairs mills or mill machinery
Shipwright-	one who designs, builds, or repairs ships
Wheelwright-	one who designs, builds, or repairs wheels, wagons, or carriages

<u>Note</u>: "Wright," coming down to us from Old English, means "workman."

Other Occupations Mentioned In The "Maryland Gazette"

Wire working business- set up by James Jolly, making sieves, safes, larders, aviaries (bird cages), wiring of windows- July,1752

Tinning & Blazing

Staymaking (See chapter on Clothing)- Corset making

Rope making- (This required a very long working space known as a "ropewalk." A Baltimore street is still named "Ropewalk Lane.")

Windmills and Tide Mills

Windmills, as well as mills having water-wheels, furnished much of the

(Continued on Page 106)

WINDMILL

MAIN GEAR - GRISTMILL

GRISTMILL

<u>Money, Manufacturing, and Trade</u> (Cont'd from Page 104)

power used in manufacturing. Tide mills, along salt-water rivers, were pow-
ered by the ebb and flow of the tide. "The huge wooden wheel turned one way
when the tide flowed into the cove, the other way when it ebbed." Typical
of the various windmills was one which was first put into use, 1760. (Riley's,
<u>The Ancient City</u>,: "It was reckoned to be the strongest and best built mill
in the country. It ground, with middling wind, twelve bushels an hour." It
stood on a spot, "Windmill Point," which is now part of the U.S. Naval
Academy grounds. Near there, the famous "Peggy Stewart Tea Party" took place-
1774 - when Anthony Stewart, owner of the ship carrying taxable tea, was
obliged to burn both ship and cargo).

As late as early Civil War days (1861), large rifle and gun factories, at
Harper's Ferry, were operated entirely by the waterpower of the Potomac River.

(Continued on next page)

A cast-iron "fireback," such as this one, (3 feet high, 2½ feet wide, 1½
inches thick) protected the bricks at the back of a fireplace against the
great heat and blackening effects of scorching fires. Most "firebacks"
were ornamental, too. "In 1719, by an act of the Assembly of Maryland, 100
acres of land was offered to anyone who would erect an iron furnace and
nine forges in the state; Principio Furnace, in Cecil County, was the first.
A furnace and a forge were and are, two different things... Iron works
were forges and some probably both."

Money, Manufacturing, and Trade (Cont'd)

Plantations Made, Or Stored, Most Of The Supplies They Needed

Planters (and even those living on small farms) tried to manufacture ("on the place") most of things they needed. This was one way of avoiding trips to the nearest store. A plantation was really somewhat like a town. It had its own workmen of different kinds, its own water supply, and most of the food and medical supplies it would need for many months. This has been well described by the son of an 18th-century Potomac River planter, thus:

"It was very much the practice with gentlemen of landed and slave estates.. so to organize them as to have considerable resources within themselves; to employ and pay but few tradesmen and to buy little or none of the coarse stuffs and materials used by them, and this practice became stronger and more general during the long period of the Revolutionary War which in great measure cut off the means of supply from elsewhere.

"Thus, my father had among his slaves carpenters, coopers, sawyers, black-smiths, tanners, curriers, shoemakers, spinners, weavers, and knitters, and even a distiller. His woods furnished timber and plank for the carpenters and coopers, and charcoal for the blacksmith; his cattle, killed for his own consumption and for sale, supplied skins for the tanners, curriers, and shoemakers, and his sheep gave wool and his fields produced cotton and flax for the weavers and spinners, and his orchards fruit for the distiller... His coopers made the hogsheads the tobacco was prized in, and the tight casks to hold the cider and other liquors...

"The blacksmiths did all the iron work required by the establishment, as making and repairing ploughs, harrows, teeth chains, etc. The spinners, weavers, and knitters made all the coarse cloths and stockings... The dis-tiller made every fall a good deal of apple, peach, and persimmon brandy. The art of distilling from grain was not then among us, and but few dis-tilleries... Moreover all the beeves and hogs for consumption for sale were driven up and slaughtered at the proper seasons, and whatever was to be preserved was salted and packed away..."

Ship Cargoes

Ocean trading was often "three cornered." Flour might be shipped to the West Indies, after which the same ship might continue by hauling rum and molasses to England, and then return from England to Maryland with a cargo containing hardware and textiles.

The cargo of a ship was usually owned by a number of persons rather than by just one individual. One person might own 1/10th, 1/20th, or 1/50th of the value of the entire cargo. One of the share-holders was usually a merchant, (called a "factor") who handled insurance, collections, storage, and finan-cing. In addition, he might arrange to haul freight for other merchants be-sides acting as a commission agent in selling various things. Regular schedules of arrival and departure were almost unknown. Quite often, the

Money, Manufacturing, and Trade (Cont'd)

Uses Of Wood

Opposite Page ▶

A) American holly, though not very strong, is tough, light, and fine-grained - well suited for making ox yokes and for cabinet work.

B) The Conestoga wagon--- "freight car of the pioneers"--- needed many different kinds of wood for its construction, including: tough white oak for its frame; gum, with unsplittable gnarly grain, for its wheel hubs; springy tough hickory for its wagon spokes, axles, and singletrees (cross-bars); and light, easily-worked poplar for boards of the body.

C) Wooden hogsheads (large casks) of tobacco could be rolled, in this manner, to the nearest wharf.

D) The wheelwright or wainwright needs all the artistry he possesses for the difficult job of making and fitting together the parts of a wheel. The rim of the wheel is shod with pieces of flat wrought iron--- fastened on while red-hot and immediately cooled in water, to prevent scorching and weakening the wooden rim. The iron, thus cooled, shrinks into place tightly, "until death do us part."

E) In his well-known poem, "The Deacon's Masterpiece, or"The Wonderful One-Hoss Shay," Oliver Wendell Holmes gives us some information about uses of wood, together with two surprising rhymes:

> ..."So the Deacon inquired of the village folk
> Where he could find the strongest oak
> That couldn't be split nor bent nor broke,-
> That was for spokes and floor and sills;
> He sent for lancewood to make the thills;
> The crossbars were ash, from the straightest trees,
> The panels of white-wood, that cuts like cheese,
> But lasts like iron from things like these;
> The hubs of logs from the 'Settler's ellum,' -
> Last of its timber,- they couldn't sell 'em...."

F) When "tonging" for oysters, Maryland's sailormen use long-handled scissors-like rakes. The two shafts (or handles) may be made from edge-grain fir or Georgia pine. A pin of dogwood (one of the heaviest and hardest woods) holds the two shafts together.

Continued from Page 107

captain and his "supercargo" (the cargo-owner's agent) simply wandered from port to port, looking for the best opportunities of buying, selling, or hauling freight.

After 1750, some of the merchants of Annapolis and Georgetown began to "carry in stock" certain imported articles for which there was a frequent

(Continued on Page 110)

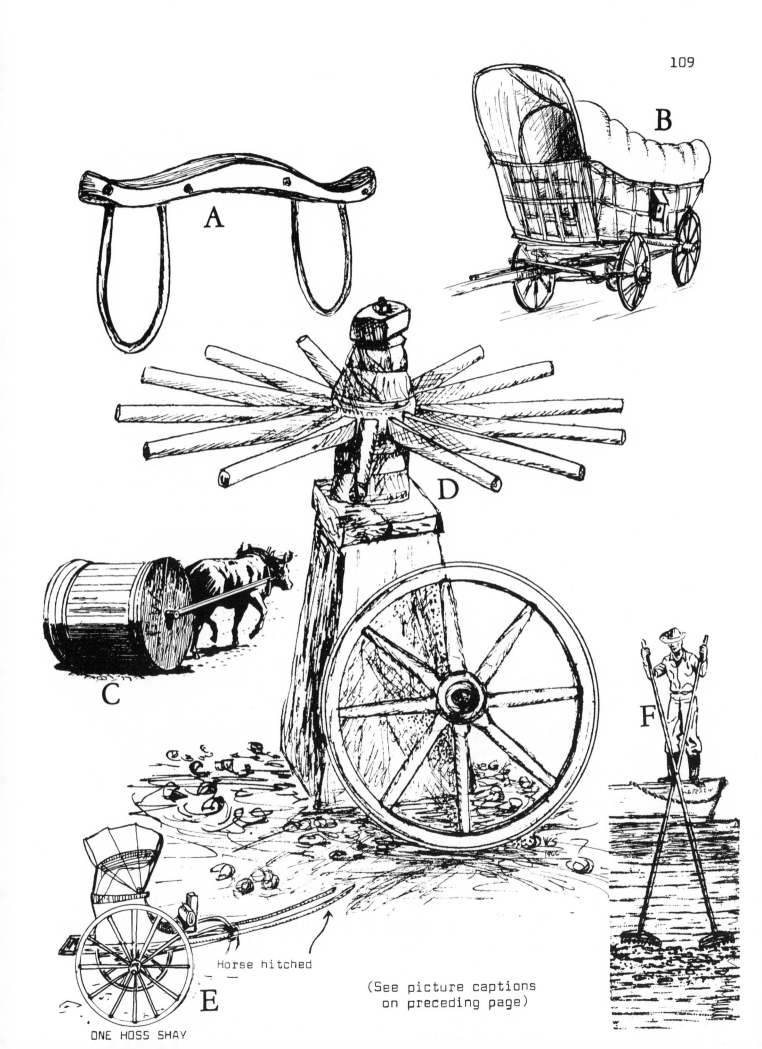

109

A

B

C

D

E

F

Horse hitched

ONE HOSS SHAY

(See picture captions
on preceding page)

Money, Manufacturing, and Trade (Cont'd)

demand; but numerous other items still had to be ordered in advance from overseas merchants or manufacturers. Trade, in Maryland, was carried on mainly through three channels:

1) the general store
2) the peddlers, who distributed drugs, small notions, and other easily-carried wares
3) fairs and markets

Markets were frequently set up near a waterfront or courthouse, on two or three days of the week. Saturdays were the most popular days. Here, farmers sold their farm produce, and here they had opportunities of buying manufactured articles.

Manufacturing

The American Revolution, which naturally brought sharp reductions in imports, had a powerful effect in encouraging manufacturing. There was not a great deal of it in Maryland, even as late as 1769. In 1772, however, the country's first umbrellas were being manufactured in Baltimore under the slogan which has continued in use to this day: "Born in Baltimore, Raised Everywhere." By 1785, John Frederick Amelung, with 68 workmen from his native city of Bremen, Germany, was establishing a glass factory near Frederick, producing glass equalling in beauty that of Venice and Bohemia. Baltimore's first sugar refinery was founded in 1796 and, by that time, many other industries had been started throughout the state.

Imports And Exports

Imports also increased after the Revolution, but mainly among articles which could not be produced here at that time. The country's principal imports, in 1790, were: dry goods; rum, brandy, and wine; tea; sugar; salt and molasses. Sugar was usually transported in barrels; molasses and tobacco were shipped in hogsheads; and wine came across the ocean in "pipes," or large casks. As for exports, North America furnished the Old World with some products formerly obtainable only at great expense from the Far East, such as rice and dyes, and others which had been either scarce or unknown, such as furs and tobacco. Finally, another branch of trade developed between the Americas and the West coast of Africa, in which rum, cloth, trinkets, and other such items were exchanged for black slaves, ivory, gold dust, ostrich feathers, and the like.

Money, Manufacturing, and Trade (Cont'd)

Many Kinds Of Money Were In Use

Although British money was the official standard for buying and selling, throughout the colonies, other kinds of money were widely used. Chief among these was the Spanish dollar-- the "piece of eight" mentioned frequently in Robert Louis Stevenson's masterpiece, <u>Treasure Island</u>. Spanish, French, and other coins had an accepted value in terms of British money. Therefore, all accounts were kept in pounds, shillings, and pence. A "piece of eight" had a value of about four shillings and sixpence. Since there was always a real scarcity of coins, tobacco was widely used in place of money throughout Maryland, for 150 years. This called for rather complicated figuring because some grades of tobacco were worth more than others.

"Tavern money" was used in various parts of the state, and was issued by taverns as a substitute for silver coins in sums of less than three or four shillings. This kind of paper money was good if the reputation of the tavern and innkeeper was good, and it was usually printed from engraved plates to guard against counterfeiting.

Because small coins were scarce, in America's early days, Spanish dollars and other large coins were cut into halves and quarters. From this custom, undoubtedly, came our name of "quarter" for a 25-cent coin.

How Coins Were "Clipped"

Even in handling coins, it was necessary to use great care to avoid being "short-changed" by the practice of "clipping." There were those who "clipped" gold and silver coins, when handling them, by filing off (and keeping) a few grains of the precious metal from each. Having this in mind, experienced merchants took to weighing coins, and allowing less value to those which were short in weight. Reeding (or "milling") the edges of American <u>silver</u> coins (but <u>not</u> nickels or pennies) is done nowadays to discourage mutilation of coins. It was also quite common for someone to cut a Spanish dollar into four quarters and then spend the "quarter dollars." (See above illustration)

In slang, today, a quarter is sometimes called "two bits." Our colonial ancestors not only cut Spanish dollars into quarters but once more into eighths. Two bits, then, were equal to one quarter. Sub-division even went beyond that, one bit being divided to make two "fips." Therefore, the expression "a fip and a bit" would mean a value of about 18¾ cents, and it was used through the late 1800's.

#########

Chapter 14

Education, Printing, And Mail Deliveries

Letters travelled slowly during the 18th century. Three or four months might pass before a planter could receive an answer to one of his letters ordering supplies from England. After that, another month might pass before a sailing vessel could bring the needed supplies, from across the

Writing Materials

Atlantic, and deliver them to the planter's own wharf. Regular schedules of sailings were almost unknown.

Lovers might be impatient in those days, but their mail travelled just as slowly. George Washington probably allowed a week or more to travel (partly by coach and partly by water) from his home in Mount Vernon, Virginia, to attend meetings held in Philadelphia. Colonel Tench Tilghman's famous speedy ride, in which he carried the news of Cornwallis' surrender from Yorktown to Philadelphia, was possible because he travelled by boat from Yorktown to Annapolis, and again from Annapolis across the Chesapeake Bay to Rock Hall. A letter travelling by this same route, in the usual fashion, would have required from one to two weeks to complete the journey.

Envelopes were not used

Envelopes were not used for enclosing letters. Instead, each letter was written on a rather large sheet of paper. This was then folded several times, and sealed on one side by means of hot sealing wax. The address was then written on the other side. A candle stood on nearly every desk, for use in melting the sealing wax.

Other Writing Materials

Blotters and blotting paper were not in use then. It was necessary to sprinkle sand on pen-and-ink writing to prevent the wet ink from smearing. (The sand used, as a general rule, was not _really_ sand. It was "pounce," an absorbent light-colored powder made from gum Sandarac, powdered charcoal, or ground cuttlefish bone). A goose quill (or wild turkey quill), which had been tapered and split, served as a pen. Not until 1809 was America's first steel pen invented, by Peregrine Williamson, a Baltimore

Education, Printing, And Mail Deliveries (Cont'd)

watchmaker. (Brass and other metallic pens, as well as quill pens, had been in use earlier overseas).

As described by lines in an old spelling book, these are the materials needed by a student: "paper, pomice, pen, ink, knife, horn, rule, plummet, wax, sand." The knife, of course, was for the purpose of sharpening, and shaping a quill pen. The plummet, a chunk of lead usually in the shape of a pyramid, was used in ruling lines on paper.

Paper, which was made from rags then, instead of from woodpulp, was scarce and it was too highly prized for children to waste it. Slates, slate-pens, and slate-pocket-books were mentioned in the advertisement of an English bookseller, as early as 1737, but it is not likely that they came into general use in America for many years afterward. Although lead pencils were advertised in Boston as early as 1740, for threepence each, they, too, were not in common use until about 1795.

Mail Deliveries

In earlier colonial times, much of the mail was carried, as a favor, by captains of ships or drivers of stage-coaches. Benjamin Franklin was appointed as Deputy Postmaster in America, during 1737, and he served as Post-master General for the colonies from 1753 until shortly before the American Revolution. Yet, during that time, many of the arrangements for carrying and delivering mail were quite informal and irregular. Contrary to present-day practice, it was the person who received a piece of mail who paid for the postage. The charge for this was anywhere from eight pence to one or two shillings. Valuable packages and especially important letters were carried, at rather high cost, by private messengers. Upon arrival, the mail would be dumped upon a table or counter, in some village store or tavern, for all to see until it had been claimed-- piece by piece. On the other hand, this way of delivering mail offered some advantages. Time and again, a ship captain would be handed a shoe so that he could show it to a boot-maker, in London. There he would explain just how the next pair of shoes should be made.

Literary "Flourishes"

Literary "flourishes," and elaborate phrases of courtesy were found in
(Continued on Page 115)

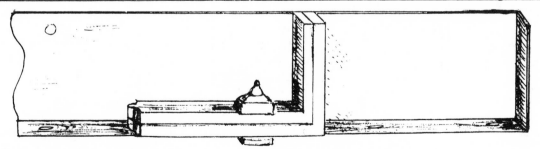

Benjamin Franklin Used This Adjustable
Metal "Composing Stick" To Set Type
For Printing

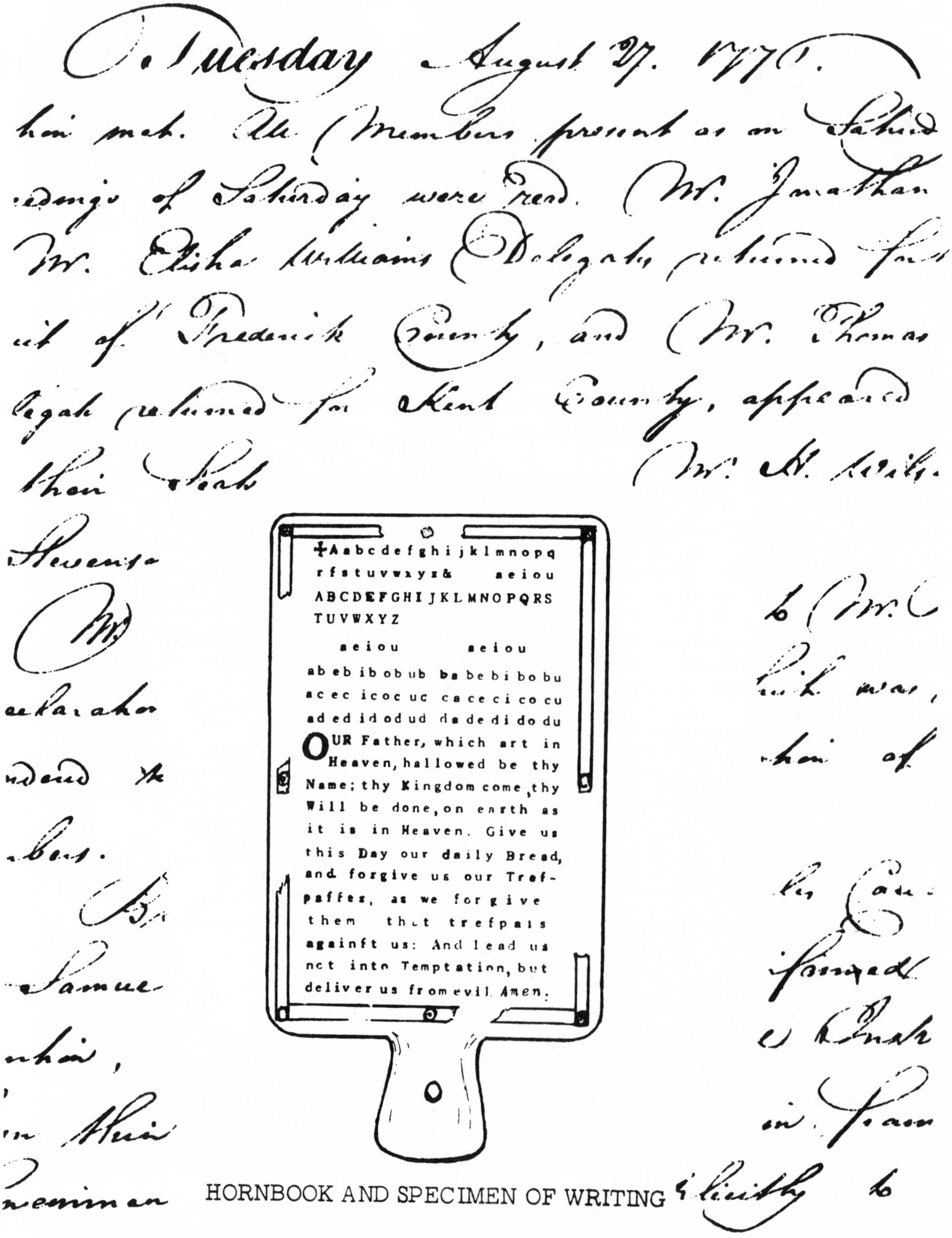
Tuesday August 27. 1776.
Aabcdefghijklmnopq
rfstuvwxyz& aeiou
ABCDEFGHIJKLMNOPQRS
TUVWXYZ
aeiou aeiou
ab eb ib ob ub ba be bi bo bu
ac ec ic oc uc ca ce ci co cu
ad ed id od ud da de di do du
OUR Father, which art in Heaven, hallowed be thy Name; thy Kingdom come, thy Will be done, on earth as it is in Heaven. Give us this Day our daily Bread, and forgive us our Trefpaffes, as we forgive them that trefpafs againft us: And lead us not into Temptation, but deliver us from evil. Amen.

HORNBOOK AND SPECIMEN OF WRITING

<u>Education, Printing, And Mail Deliveries</u> (Cont'd from Page 113)

all letters, and even in advertisements. Very common in letters, as "complimentary closes," were such phrases as "Your humble servant" and "Your obedient servant." Other phrases such as "I beg of you" were liberally used.

Newspapers And Printing

By gradual stages, printing began to flourish during the 18th century. A printing press was in operation at St. Mary's City "at least as early as 1689." This was apparently used mainly for producing pamphlets, small advertisements, and such items.

Maryland's first successful newspaper, the <u>Maryland Gazette</u>, was published as a weekly by William Parks, Printer of the Province in Annapolis, during 1727. About 1734, the paper was discontinued for a time when Mr. Parks decided that Virginia offered a better field for his talents. He went to Williamsburg to start the <u>Virginia Gazette</u> and a printing shop.

In 1745, the <u>Maryland Gazette</u> was revived by Jonas Green, who then had two positions, as Postmaster and also as Printer to the Province. This weekly newspaper made progress under Mr. Green's management. After his death, publication was continued by his widow. Files of its copies, preserved in various ways, have served as valuable historical documents and reference sources, holding a mirror to much of the colony's most interesting aspects.

A New Postal System

It appears that Benjamin Franklin, (though one of America's greatest inventors and leaders) should be given only a part of the credit for

(Continued on next page)

Religious activities in most homes centered around the family Bible. In addition, it usually contained a complete record of births, baptisms, weddings, and deaths. For this reason, family Bibles were frequently accepted as evidence in courts of law.

Education, Printing, And Mail Deliveries (Cont'd)

starting our postal system. A Baltimore printer, William Goddard, hired "post riders" (men on horseback to carry messages and newspapers) in 1773. Items of news were brought without delay directly to his newspaper, the Maryland Journal. This led to starting the "Constitutional Post Office," 1774. Our present postal system grew from this.

Records, And How They Were Kept

Wills, mortgages, and many other 18th-century records were kept in boxes, and chests stored in vaults. Less important papers were stored on shelves or in cupboards, where they soon became covered with dust, or were nibbled by mice. Copies of all documents had to be made patiently by hand, using pen and ink. Chests were opened and closed by using large-size heavy keys. There was no carbon paper or other such means of making copies. One of the chief duties of a lawyer's clerk, seated on a high stool at a high desk, was the work of writing or copying wills, deeds, contracts, and other documents.

Education

In education, Maryland children of the 18th century were divided into "upper class" and "lower class." Rich people could afford to engage tutors or to send their children to foreign countries for further study. Those from working class families were fortunate if able to attend one of the few county "free schools." (They were not entirely "free," since parents of students shared certain expenses). Many a farm boy or girl acquired his or her education entirely at home (an education limited to elementary reading, writing, and "ciphering"- simple arithmetic). There were only about ten or eleven colleges in all America before 1800. Among them were St. John's College, Annapolis,(1784) and Washington College,(1782) in Chestertown.

The "Hornbook" - A Means Of Learning ABC's

Generally, a child's education began by making use of a "hornbook,"from which they learned their letters and some simple spelling.(See Page 114).It was actually not a book, consisting of a wooden paddle on which was fastened a piece of paper. On this were printed letters of the alphabet, simple syllables and, finally, the Lord's Prayer, covered by a thin piece of yellowish horn, to protect the contents.

Geography

Geography was "an accomplishment rather than a necessary study." Charles Willson Peale's advertisement in a Maryland Gazette issue of 1745 reads: "At Kent County School, Chestertown,Maryland, young gentlemen are boarded and taught the Greek and Latin tongues, writing, arithmetic, merchant's accounts, surveying, navigation, and the use of the globes by the largest and most accurate pair in America: also any other parts of the mathematics. N.B. Young gentlemen can be instructed in fencing and dancing by very good masters."

Schooling Without Schools

In place of schooling, a great deal of practical "how to do it" knowledge was gathered by almost everyone. A boy knew the best ways of doing farm work, and how to handle an axe, shoot, and fish. He was well prepared for all pioneering and exploring. Likewise, girls acquired a great deal of household knowledge. From necessity and daily occupation, most children learned to be industrious, to be thrifty, and to have initiative.

As a center of culture, Baltimore began to go beyond Annapolis in the late 1700's. This city had a daily newspaper by 1791 and, in 1796, a semi-public library. From this time on, learning flourished. Books were more plentiful, and the ability to read and write became more common.

#######

Chapter 15

Medicine, And Health

Being ill, in colonial days, was a most unpleasant experience. Medicines, especially the "home remedies," were prepared with the idea that the more disagreeable the taste, the more likely the cure. Anesthetics were unknown. Not until 1846 was ether used for this purpose. Cocaine, as a local pain-killer, was not introduced until 1855. Consequently, every surgical operation was very painful.

Dental Treatment

Dentistry was largely a matter of pulling teeth. A set of dental plates made after the Revolution for George Washington was carved from ivory and fastened to gold plates. He owned three other sets of dental plates, one of which was made from wood. Not many others were in use, throughout the colonies. Only rich people could afford to have them made.

In many instances, "the cure was worse than the disease." An example of this was the medical procedure of "blood-letting," or bleeding, as the accepted treatment for a long list of ailments. George Washington's physicians gave him this treatment during his last illness (together with a gargle of vinegar and sage tea). It hastened his death, if it did not actually cause it, some people think.

Doctors Sometimes Were Druggists

Hospitals, with some few exceptions, did not exist. Medical treatment, therefore, was usually given in the patient's home. The doctor, himself, might actually divide his time between his medical duties and some other activity, such as operating an apothecary's shop (drug store). (The noted Dr. Hugh Mercer, in Fredericksburg, Virginia, conducted an apothecary's shop which adjoined his medical office and surgery). Furthermore, there were not many doctors. Because travel was slow, there was nearly always some delay in bringing the doctor to the patient, or the patient to the doctor. In 1787, life expectancy of males in the United States was only about 35 years. This compares with 70 years, today, (women, today: 75 years).

The present-day practice of having yearly medical examinations, or "check-ups," was non-existent during the 1700's. When a doctor's services were required, it was because of great suffering. Indeed, the doctor ordinarily was not called until a number of "home remedies" (such as boneset tea, sage tea, sarsaparilla, or sassafras juice) had been tried. Prescriptions for such remedies were passed from one family to another, such as cooking recipes. (Some people still use them, today. Leaves or roots of plants used in medicines were ground to a powder by using a mortar and pestle. See illustration- next page).

Medicine, And Health (Cont'd)

The childhood disease of rickets, seldom found today, was frequent then, because children didn't get any citrus fruits; didn't drink much milk; and didn't get much sunshine during six months of the year.

"Home Remedies"

Among "genuine patent medicines" listed in an advertisement of the late 1700's are:"James's analeptic pills and fever powders, essence of peppermint, British oil, Anderson's pills, Steer's opodeldoc for sprains, rheumatism and bruises, cephalic snuff for head-ache, lozenges of toulo for colds, coughs, and consumptions, Hill's balsam of honey, Stoughton's bitters, and court plaister." A celebrated remedy for many ailments was offered by the anodyne necklace, which was simply worn around the neck. Great healing powers were claimed for it.

Lessons Learned From The Indians

It is only fair to say that the white man learned much, from the Indians of both North and South America, concerning plant material having medicinal uses. Quinine (from the cinchona trees of Central and South America), witch hazel, lobelia, and bloodroot, were quickly adopted into medical practice of the Old and New Worlds. Tobacco, as a narcotic and in surgery, was used often before it was widely adopted for smoking.

Smallpox

Although their portraits never show it, George Washington and many other colonial notables had the pock marks of smallpox on their faces. This was a matter of personal appearance which portrait painters politely ignored when painting a picture. Louis XIV of France had smallpox, and Louis XV died of it.

Inoculation Against Smallpox

A method of inoculation against this deadly disease was introduced into England, during 1717, by Lady Mary Montague, wife of the British Ambassador to Turkey. The method produced only a mild case of smallpox, rarely fatal. After a few days of unpleasant symptoms, it gave protection against catching the disease. The first such inoculation in North America was given in 1769, by Dr. Henry Stevenson, one of the founders of Baltimore, and organizer of the city's first medical society. Also in 1769, the first U.S. smallpox hospital was founded in Baltimore. This led to establishment of the University of Maryland Medical School.

Vaccinations

Happy news for everyone was the introduction of successful vaccination for smallpox by Edward Jenner, of Gloucestershire, England, in 1798. Thomas Jefferson arranged vaccination for the members of his family,and many thousands of others did the same.

Instruction

There were few schools of medicine or law in 18th-century America. Therefore young men wishing to learn these professions worked and studied in the offices of well-known doctors or lawyers. This, then, was the state of health and medicine in Maryland during the 1700's. Nature, as always, was the great healer.

######

Some Uses Of

P L A N T   M A T E R I A L S

Some of the items listed below may sound familiar because individuals, physicians, and drug manufacturers of today have followed various customs established by our forefathers. 20th-century "miracle drugs" have not entirely replaced certain leaves, roots, stems, or flowers which may be growing in or near your own backyard. "Nature's medicine chest" - of yesterday and today - has included a great many more things than can be mentioned here. Indeed, two, three, or four different kinds of plants have been useful, occasionally, to obtain the same basic effect. A single plant variety may have been known by several different names. Several different parts of the same plant, now, as then, have different medicinal uses.

Food Substitutes For	Item Used	Part Used	How Used
Coffee	Acorns	Whole	Roasted & ground
"	Chicory	Root	" "
Chocolate	Black Sorghum	Seeds	Crushed
Yeast	Peaches	Leaves	Dried
"	Hops	Leafy cone	In beverages
Salad greens	Burdock	Leaf stems	Gathered in early spring, peeled like rhubarb.
" "	Dandelion	Leaves	Raw or cooked, in early spring.

To Repel			
Moths & Ants	Gray Southernwood	Branches	Placed around the house.
Flies	Asparagus	Fern	Hung in bunches around the house.
Mosquitos	Pennyroyal	Bunches	Hung from rafters.
Mice	Spearmint	Leaves	Bunches packed with clothing
Dandruff	Sage	Leaves	Brewed, and applied to head.

Miscellaneous			
Ink Making	Pokeweed	Leaves	As a liquid
Pillow stuffing	Cotton Weed	Flower	For pillows
Soap substitute	Soapwort	Flower	Makes lather (without water)
Gunpowder	White Willow Tree	Charcoal	Mixed with other ingredients

Note:
Insecticide: Sprinkling a liquid from the roots of the May Apple (sketch) on potato plants, may be looked upon as an early use of insecticide.

Chlorophyll, a familiar name to us today, is made from Stinging Nettle. Other claims for its value: Cure for burns; and when young shoots are boiled and eaten, it is a remedy for scurvy.

Chapter 16

Transportation

There were times during severe winters when the Chesapeake Bay was frozen solidly from shore to shore. This actually helped land transportation, instead of hindering it. Skates and sleds travelled over the ice at will, as long as the cold weather lasted. Two barrel staves, one fastened to each foot, enabled many a person to glide along on the ice or snow.

Generally, the roads were terrible in the full sense of the word. The average colonial road was a dirt road. Clouds of dust were stirred from it in hot dry weather, but it became a muddy trap in wet weather.

Travel By Water Was Preferred

It was for this reason that the colonists travelled by boat as much as possible. A journey of thirty miles by water was not only quicker than a journey of ten miles by land, but also safer, and far more pleasant. Because of the expense involved in draining, bridging, or going around marshes (as well as in grading and paving) few good roads were built until the 1800's. There were not many bridges in the American colonies, so that shallow rivers had to be "forded" (ridden across at a place where the water was not deep). Deeper ones were crossed on ferries, each of which might charge a shilling to carry a coach or similar vehicle. The cost of land transportation was very high, except for light articles having small bulk, such as tea. For all these reasons, and many more, numerous travellers between north and south took ship between Rock Hall and Annapolis, or from "Head of Elk" (near what is now Elkton), to ports in Virginia. The road of water was the route of few delays. It was the one of least danger, as well as the one on which great loads could be carried cheaply; and Maryland was fortunate in having a great many long waterways.

Horseback Travel Was Popular

Horseback riding was preferred by many travellers, as a means of avoiding the "shaking up" and other discomforts experienced by stage-coach passengers. Oftentimes, a rider would lead a packhorse carrying considerable quantities of goods. Now and then, a party of four travellers would make use of only one horse during a journey. Two men would mount the horse and ride a mile or two, leaving the two others to follow on foot. Then the first two riders would dismount, tie the horse by the roadside and continue on foot. The other two, after reaching the animal and mounting would overtake them. In this manner, "turn and turn about," the journey continued.

(Continued on Page 122)

A "corduroy" road could be built through swamp country, by laying
logs on which dirt was then packed down.

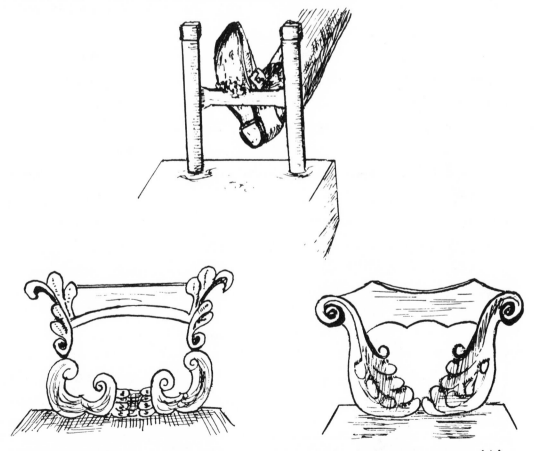

Foot-scrapers were often quite ornamental, but were necessities---
to scrape mud from shoes before entering a building.

Transportation (Cont'd from Page 120)

Corduroy Roads

Here and there "corduroy roads" were built. This was a means of guarding against "washouts." Many small logs were placed side by side. Over this a layer of dirt, about three or four inches thick, was spread. The logs were intended to provide sound foundation. Actually, however, much of the dirt would wash away, so that travel over the road log base produced numerous jolts and bumps. These very quickly "shook the coaches and wagons to pieces." The National Road (Cumberland westward, 1808) and the somewhat earlier "post roads" (for mail and passenger stagecoaches) were, of course, rather good highways.

Two-Notch And Three-Notch Roads

A system of highway marking, according to a law passed in 1704, required that any road leading to a ferry, court house, or church should be "marked on both sides of the road with two notches." A road to a ferry was to be marked "with three notches at equal Distance at the entrance into the same." To this day, the road leading north from Point Lookout is known as the "Three-Notched Road."

Stagecoaches & Conestoga Wagons

A stagecoach, between 1750 and the Revolution, more nearly resembled a "box on wheels" than anything else. It was after the war that these vehicles became more comfortable and more attractive. The Conestoga wagons were, of course, the "freight cars" of colonial Maryland. Later, with some changes, they were the "prairie schooners" of the westward pioneers. (See Page 109). They originated in the Conestoga Valley near Lancaster, Pennsylvania, and weighed about 3,500 pounds when empty. Yet the woods employed in building them were as light as possible without sacrificing strength. When loaded, they could carry as much as 10,000 pounds! (or in the language of the old wagon drivers,) "a hundred hundred!" Traditionally, the lower part of a Conestoga wagon was painted blue. The removable side board, above this, was painted red. The white canvas tops, stretched over a wooden framework, produced an attractive red-white-and-blue color scheme. Usually they were pulled by six horses.

Lodging For The Night

Inns and taverns were quite important matters in journeys of any distance. Some of them were called "ordinaries." In any case, they were the local centers of social life and political discussion. Gambling, card-playing, bowling, and billiards were popular amusements - either in them or nearby. Since all kinds of notices were fastened near the entrances of most inns, they frequently resembled bulletin boards. A large public assembly room, including a bar, for serving drinks, was always a prominent feature,

Transportation (Cont'd)

including a large fireplace, chairs, and tables. The dining room was usually a separate room. The stables had provision for everything except private vehicles, until about 1750. This was because only travellers by stagecoach, or on horseback and foot, were expected.

Under the unwritten laws of hospitality, each innkeeper considered it his duty to provide shelter for all who came to his door. Therefore, when a traveller found that all the beds were already occupied, he simply spread his blankets on the floor of the public room and made himself as comfortable as possible. This was not at all unusual. Those were the days when a meal meant "all that a man wanted to eat." Second and third helpings of food, tea, coffee or milk were usually offered without comment.

Ferry Boats

Every colonial traveller soon encountered ferries, and learned that they did not operate on a regular schedule. Their comings and goings were fitted into other activities which might be of interest to the ferryman - such as fishing or working at a trade. The ferries ranged in size from large sailing vessels on down to canoes or rowboats suitable for foot-travellers. If the ferry was not large enough to accommodate both horses and wagons, the horses would swim. Many times the ferry would consist of two or more canoes lashed together,(See illustration). Sometimes it would be a flat-boat which was slowly but steadily pulled across the stream by a rope or cable. Now and then, a ferry would land on a sandbar, or farther downstream than the ferryman had intended. In such cases, everybody got wet and a few tempers may have been heated up before getting back to the main road.

Delaware and Chesapeake Bay Boats

The sloop was a popular means of transportation on inland waters, as it is today. In earlier colonial days it was referred to as "shallop." The word evidently changed, by degrees, to "sloop." Such distinctive types of Chesapeake Bay boats as the bugeye, pungy, and skipjack were not developed until well into the 1800's. In addition to sloops, popular types of boats on the Chesapeake Bay and its tributary rivers were schooners of various kinds, long-boats, and log canoes. Oftentimes, the construction of these, and larger vessels, was begun in autumn, some distance from the water. When work was finished, during winter, these were hauled by oxen, over the snow or ice, for launching at the water's edge. For ocean travel, such old types of sailing vessels as barks, barkentines,brigs, brigantines, ketches (or"catches"), and snows (a type of ship resembling a brig) were used.

(Continued on Page 125)

A DECK LAID OVER TWO CANOES

MARYLAND SHIPYARD (prior to the Revolution)
(Ships left to right are: Snow, brig, and sloop)

<u>Transportation</u> (Cont'd from Page 123)

The Coming Of The Steamboat

As the end of the century approached, there came a revolutionary development in water travel--- the steamboat. On December 3, and again on December 11, 1787, James Rumsey operated a steamboat driven by a power pump, on the Potomac River. In 1791, he was granted a patent for it, but other types of steamboats became more popular. (Rumsey was born, 1743, in Cecil County).

Virginia, Pennsylvania and Maryland Shipbuilding

Some writers seem to think that shipbuilding south of New York was not important, in colonial days. This is not true. In his book,"The History of American Sailing Ships," Mr. Howard I Chapelle says: "Virginia and Pennsylvania, as well as Maryland, had well-developed shipbuilding industries by 1700... If the southern vessels were not so numerous or were not built so early as those of New England, it can be said that they developed in design so rapidly as to outstrip their competitors in reputation by the time of the American Revolution."

P L A C E S   T O   V I S I T

Matters of local interest are rather well covered by county or community historical societies and libraries. Obviously the historical societies of Virginia, Pennsylvania, Maryland and Delaware have much to offer. But there are others listed here:

Exhibits and dioramas on "Everyday Life in Early America," 2nd floor, National Museum of History and Technology, Smithsonian Institution, Washington, D.C.

The Jonathan Hager House, with its museum, and nearby country store, Hagerstown; and the Shriver Homestead, Union Mills--- both listed in greater detail in the chapter on <u>Houses</u>. (nominal admission).

The Carroll County Farm Museum, near Westminster, Maryland (nominal fee).

The Chesapeake Bay Maritime Museum, St. Michaels; and the Oxford, Maryland,Museum. (nominal admission)

The Hammond-Harwood House, Annapolis (admission)

Museum, U.S. Naval Academy, Annapolis (free)

Old Salem, Winston-Salem, N.C. Old buildings, workshops, craftsmen, etc. (admission)

Jamestown and Colonial Williamsburg, Virginia (admission)

The Frigate <u>Constellation</u>, Pratt Street, and the nearby Flag House, at Albemarle Street, Baltimore. (nominal admission)

St. Mary's City (Maryland's First Capital, 1634) now being preserved and developed (with significant displays of artifacts) by the St. Mary's City Commission (free); and

Sotterley (also in Maryland's "Mother County") a "working tobacco plantation" dating back to colonial days, facing the Patuxent River. (Admission; open June thru Sept.).

▲▲▲▲▲▲▲▲▲▲▲▲▲▲▲▲▲▲▲▲▲▲▲▲▲▲▲▲▲▲▲▲▲▲▲▲▲▲

Some Of The Things Which Did Not Exist Before 1800

adding machine (1820); aluminum products (1825)- Denmark; aspirin (1893)

*baking powder; barbed wire (1867); bathtubs (built-in); bicycles

carbon paper; chewing gum; clothes cupboards (built-in); covered bridges

department stores; dry cleaning process (1849)- France; dynamite

elastic rubber bands; envelopes (probably used only rarely); ether

filing cabinets (vertical); forks (with four tines, about 1800- two or
   three before that)

galvanized iron; gasoline;and gasoline engines; glass (heat-resistant)

#income tax; iodine (1812)

kerosene (and, of course, kerosene lamps or stoves)

*Levis,(or blue jeans); linoleum

matches;

oranges and lemons as part of regular diet (delicacies before 1832);

packaging (individual) for most food products; paper towels; photography;
   postal cards (1869)- Austria

quinine (isolated 1820)

rifles (repeating); rubber hose (garden)

safes (fire-resistive); sewing machine (1829)-France; shoes (lefts &
   rights- 1800); stethoscope (1819)

telephone & telegraph; tinware (did not replace iron or brass until 1815)
   toilets (flush); typewriters

vaseline; vulcanized rubber boots and overshoes

*weather bureau

─────────────

*Baking powder (not developed until about 1850). Previously cooks used
   baking soda, saleratus, pearlash, and eggs to "make cakes light"

*Levis: In the days before the 1849 Gold Rush to California, "working clothes "
   were simply "old clothes." Levi Strauss, a Jewish immigrant from Bavaria,
   could recognize an opportunity when he saw one. He had tenting material
   which was not selling well, but quickly arranged to make long-lasting
   hard-wearing denim pants, from it--- and his "work clothes" began to
   sell like "hot cakes" to miners who needed something that would"wear."
   Noticing a blacksmith riveting some back-pockets with black iron nails,
   Levi adopted the idea, with improvements,using non-rusting copper rivets.

*Weather Bureau forecasts were not an official service of the U.S.Government
   until the late 1800's. Beginning about 1880, the gifted French-born
   Julien P. Friez outfitted and operated, in Baltimore, this country's
   first privately-owned weather observatory, named Belfort.

U.S.

Some Of The Things Which Did Exist Before The End Of The 18th Century

almanacs;

balloon ascensions (1782)- France; barometers; bifocal eyeglasses

canning of food (between 1795 & 1810, by Appert,- France); cement; circular
    saw; circus performances;*clapboard (house siding); cotton gin (1793,
    Eli Whitney,- U.S.)

dictionaries; door-bells; dumb-waiters

encyclopedias

*felt

gas lighting (city), 1793- Great Britain;

lightning rods; lithography (1798)- Germany

magnifying glasses; mirrors (wall)

nail-making machine (1790)

parachute (1783)- France; parasol- China; Patent Office, U.S.

rocking chair (1775)- U.S.

screw propeller (1785)- Great Britain; *slip covers; spinning & carding
    machinery (1764)- U.S.;*stucco (house siding); submarines & mines (1776-77)
    David Bushnell, U.S.;

telescopes; thermometers; threshing machine (1786)- Great Britain

*toothbrushes

Venetian blinds

wallpaper

*window screens

———————

*Clapboard: This is old, though muscle-power, wedges, and either mallets or
  axes were needed to split it from logs, in earlier times.

*Felt: This is an ancient material, apparently known in Homer's time. When
  the Crusaders found the Saracens using it for tents, they introduced it into
  Europe. The word "felt" comes from the Dutch, vilt,(a fabric made without
  weaving by the use of rolling, beating, or pressure, causing fibers of wool,
  hair, or fur to interlock).

*Slip covers: Yellow buckram cases for an armchair were made as early as 1611
  by an English upholsterer.

*Stucco: This is quite old. There is evidence to show that 16th-century Indians
  made it, using sand and lime (from oyster shells). The mansion of the
  Ridgely family, Hampton (completed in 1783 just north of Towson, had stucco
  exterior walls, as it does today).

*Toothbrushes: Though they were not in common use for some time, a few have
  been found during archeological work at the Jonathan Hager House, built,
  (1739-40), at Hagerstown, Maryland.

*Window Screens:(Maryland Gazette,1752)-"James Jolly makes..wiring of windows"

List of Some Useful Publications

The American Colonies: 1492-1750, by Marcus W. Jernigan.

The American Colonies in the Seventeenth Century, by Herbert L. Osgood.

The American Colonies in the Eighteenth Century, by Herbert L. Osgood.

The Architecture of Colonial America, by Harold D. Eberlein.

Child Life in Colonial Days, by Alice Morse Earle.

Colonial Folkways (Chronicles of America), by Charles M. Andrews.

Colonial Living, written and illustrated by Edwin Tunis.

The Dutch and Quaker Colonies, by John Fiske.

Everyday Things in American Life: 1607 - 1776, by William Chauncy Langdon, Macmillan Publishing Company, New York, 1937. Reprinted 1981.

First People of Maryland, by Hettie Ballweber, archaeologist, Maryland Historical Press, Lanham, MD, 1987.

History of Colonial America, by Oliver Perry Chitwood.

Home Life in Colonial Days, by Alice Morse Earle.

The Homes of Our Ancestors, R. T. H. Halsey and Elizabeth Tower.

Indians of the Tidewater County of Maryland, Virginia, North Carolina and Delaware, by Thelma G. Ruskin. Maryland Historical Press, Lanham, MD, 1990 2d ed.

The Maryland Colony, by F. Van Wyck Mason. Crowell-Collier Press, the Macmillan Company, Toronto, Ontario, Canada. 1969.

Old Virginia and Her Neighbors, by John Fiske.

Tobacco Coast, by Arthur P. Middleton.

It took a great deal of work to clear fields for crops in colonial days. There were no chain saws or bulldozers! Men used axes and hand-pulled saws. Oxen and horses helped pull stumps.

Winter was often a hard time in colonial days. Yet, there were cozy times, too. What do you see in this picture that colonial farmers did not have? The wire fence? Correct!

J. H. Cromwell photograph.

At Linchester, Maryland, near Preston this old mill stands. It is said to be the oldest privately-owned business in the United States. Caroline County records mention it as early as 1681. Water used to turn the old mill wheel.

J. H. Cromwell photograph

######